Pressing Questions

EXPLORATIONS

IN SOCIOLOGY

**Kevin
McDonald**

LONGMAN

An imprint of
Addison Wesley Longman

Addison Wesley Longman Australia Pty Limited
95 Coventry Street
South Melbourne 3205 Australia

Offices in Sydney, Brisbane and Perth, and associated companies
throughout the world.

Cover design by Carol Hudson
Text design by Bookhouse Digital, Sydney
Set in 11/13 pt Gill Sans
Printed in Malaysia through Longman Malaysia, PP

National Library of Australia
Cataloguing-in-Publication data

McDonald, Kevin.
Pressing questions: explorations in sociology.

Issue 1.
ISBN 0 582 81162 7.

1. Sociology. 2. Newspapers - Sections, columns, etc. -
Sociology. 3. Sociology. 4. Sociology - Problems, exercises, etc.
I. Title.

070.449301076

Contents

Introduction

Sociology is the study of how we shape the social world, and how it shapes us. Once this was more or less straightforward. Sociologists studied societies, some emphasising institutions, roles and norms, while others emphasised questions of social class. Now we are experiencing bewildering social change. National societies, once the framework for sociological study, seem to be dissolving into global flows. Once stable identities such as class and family are giving way to new and often difficult-to-chart experiences. New patterns of work are emerging, and new technologies are redefining who we are; the meaning of the life course is changing. Our selfhood, and the way we relate to others and even to our bodies, all seem to be in a process of rapid, and uncertain, transformation. As older national societies cease to be the framework of the world we live in, new questions are emerging, new terrains of the social are coming into being. This is the terrain of the discipline of sociology.

First year sociology aims to give you a sense of sociology's landscape. The Marxist tradition tends to focus on economic change and class, while Durkheimian sociology explores the way we constitute shared symbolic worlds, in particular through ritual. Interactionist sociology underlines the way we constitute ourselves through communication with others. Weberian sociology emphasises the tensions within social action, in particular between instrumental action and action shaped by values. Feminist sociology underlines the place of gender in domains as diverse as the family and technology. Emerging postmodern themes underline a shift from structure to surface in areas from image to selfhood.

These are just some of the landmarks that first year sociology introduces you to. In later years you will explore these in more depth. Then the grounding in core frameworks that you develop in first year is crucial, when you will have to decide whether to explore, say, a workplace, in terms of face-to-face interaction, or class structure, or gender relations, or symbolic structures.

First year sociology introduces you to at times a bewildering array of concepts. The best way to make these your own, and to come to some sense of their possibilities and their limits, is to use them. While your textbook introduces major sociological frameworks and concepts, *Pressing Questions* aims at beginning to help you *use* these to explore dimensions of the social world. It is a first step in moving from learning *about* sociology to beginning to *do* sociology. This means learning to become critical and creative, to look beyond the taken-for-granted, to begin to explore social dilemmas, to begin to recognise social structures, social creativity and action.

Pressing Questions allows you to use sociological concepts as lenses to explore the social world through engaging with extracts from major Australian newspapers. It aims at introducing you to reading 'between the lines' by bringing together snap-shots of social life and key sociological concepts. It is organised in sections which parallel most first year textbooks.

In each section you will find press articles, followed by two types of questions. The *concepts* questions help you to make sure you understand key sociological concepts through using them to explore the articles. Each concept is italicised, and a brief definition is offered in the glossary at the end of the book.

These are followed by a question that sets up a problem for you to explore. Sometimes this involves exploring ABS data, or looking up a CD-ROM, or exploring Internet sites. But most involve undertaking exploratory interviews, and ask you to interpret the results and present these to your tutorial. If you decide to undertake these, you will need to make sure that you have *informed consent* from the people that you interview, and that you do not enter situations that potentially put your respondents or yourself at risk. You will need to be aware of your university's guidelines regarding this kind of fieldwork at undergraduate level, and to spend time in tutorials exploring issues involved in ethical fieldwork before undertaking any of those exercises.

How to use this book

This book complements major first year sociology textbooks used in Australia, and its structure generally parallels those texts. It is designed to be used collectively, in tutorials or study groups. But you can use it individually to parallel work you are doing in class. It can also be used in introductory methods subjects aimed at developing the skills of creatively reading social experiences and learning to construct research questions.

The sequence of material follows M. Haralambos et al., *Sociology: Themes and Perspectives, Australian Edition* (Melbourne: Addison Wesley Longman, 1996). I have called the exercise section 'Over to you'. Most of these exercises involve preparation and reading, and the time involved in fieldwork. If you are to use them, you will need to choose a theme well in advance to allow time to work on them.

Drawing on press material has allowed some areas to be explored more easily than others, and I am particularly keen to receive feedback, from both staff and students, about the material presented here and the sorts of questions developed. I can be contacted at k.mcdonald@politics.unimelb.edu.au.

Acknowledgements

The publisher and author would like to thank the following for permission to reproduce copyright material: *The Age, Arena Magazine, The Australian, Australian Financial Review, Business Review Weekly, The Dominion, Sydney Morning Herald, The Sunday Age*, Deirdre Macken (senior writer at the *Sydney Morning Herald*), Michael Lynch, Ian Verrender, Melissa Sweet (medical writer at the *Sydney Morning Herald*), Steve Dow, Marion Downey, Darren Gray, Helen Hawkes, Janet McCalman, Stephen Long, Jean Hillier, Kate Nancarrow, Megan Jones, Bettina Arndt, Paul Davies (physicist and author), Alicia Larriera (health writer at the *Sydney Morning Herald*), Narelle Hooper, Gretchen Miller, Nikki Barrowclough, Nicole Brady, Madeleine Bunting, John Carroll (author of *Humanism: The Wreck of Western Culture*, Fontana 1993), Adele Horin, Helen Pitt, Debra Jopson, Colin Tatz, Caroline Milburn, Ben Mitchell, Geoffrey Barker, Judith Brett, Stephen Graham, Sybil Nolan, Ali Gripper, Andrew Hornery, Kathryn House, Erin Kennedy, Michael O'Meara, Sonia Syvret, Jane Cadzow, Ron Tandberg, Cathy Wilcox, Peter Nicholson and Bruce Petty.

Kevin McDonald
Sociology Program
University of Melbourne

■ Class and social polarisation

A city divided

By DEIRDRE MACKEN

Sydney is a fractured city, split by social, economic, geographic and even psychological factors. For its more fortunate residents this may not appear such a problem but, as Deirdre Macken reports, eventually we all pay for the burdens of the great divide.

Geographically, the west of Sydney starts at Parramatta. Demographically, it begins just outside Homebush. Culturally, the west starts at Auburn's mosque. But, in effect, Sydney's west starts where the money runs out, where the jobs get scarce, where the resources get stretched and the rest of Sydney loses interest.

The west has always been Sydney's poor cousin, beyond the reach of the sea breezes and largesse of the city, but it is becoming a distant relative that shares little more than a road map with its elite eastern neighbourhood. Sydney is being split down its middle by the gentrification of the inner city, the broader polarisation of society, greater competition for government resources and seismic economic forces that have built an international city at the core and a rust belt on the rim.

Statistically, the dividing line between the haves and have-nots runs from Castle Hill in the north to the airport. On either side of this skewered east–west axis are 'two armies confronting each other', says the social economist Phil Raskall, who until recently headed the Social Policy Research Centre at the University of NSW.

So estranged are the two sides of Sydney that children are growing up in social enclaves; youth no longer travel from west to east for either work or leisure; mobility from the cheap housing belt of the west to the expensive east is confined to the most affluent and, most importantly, the east's decision-makers rarely venture into the suburban heartland.

As the self-described cultural analyst Dave McCaughan from the McCann-Erickson advertising agency says: 'The only time Sydney's elite see the west is through their windscreens on the annual trip to the snow.' Sydney never was an egalitarian city, but it has never been so divided.

Socially, the west and south-west region is closer to Adelaide than it is to central Sydney; spatially, the great suburban sprawl is now the size of Perth and, for all the attention it receives, it might as well be in Western Australia.

The polarisation of east and west is set against the backdrop of a dramatic increase in inequality in Sydney in the past 15 years. According to Raskall's research, during this time Sydney has increased its share of both rich and poor, compared to other cities, and has become the most unequal city in Australia. Within Sydney, this disparity has been amplified. Fifteen years ago the city's top 10 per cent had an average income 47 per cent higher than the bottom decile. Now they have an income 77 per cent greater than the poorest.

That Sydney barometer, average house prices, tells the same story. In the past 15 years, prices on the outer rim have increased at only two-thirds the rate (109 per cent) of

those in the inner city (150 per cent). So whereas the average house price on the outer rim sat at $75,000 in 1981 compared with $115,000 for a house in the centre, today the average house on the outer is worth less than half ($180,000) that of an inner-city house ($400,000).

On the social atlas of Sydney, the hot spots for high-income earners, well-educated, managerial, DINKs and employed are found in the east (with the exception of the Georges River area). The hot spots for low-income earners, tradespeople, young families, those without qualifications and unemployed belong to the west.

If the geographic distribution of unemployment is colour-coded on the atlas, half the west flares with pinks (10–26 per cent unemployment) and reds (26 per cent-plus unemployment) while the east records hot spots only in the inner west and eastern beaches.

The growing disparity in employment and wages between rich and poor neighbourhoods has also been documented by Professor Bob Gregory, an economist at the Australian National University, who found that income in the top 5 per cent of neighbourhoods has risen 23 per cent while those in the bottom 5 per cent have dropped 23 per cent. Male employment levels have fallen twice as fast in poor neighbourhoods than in the top ones, and female employment levels in the poorest areas have dropped 40 per cent while in the most affluent areas they have increased 10 per cent.

The result of these unemployment ghettos, Gregory says, is a ▶

society that just drifts in different directions. 'When one part (of society) is busily employed, earning lots of money, and the other part is unemployed, you must expect the beliefs and attitudes of the two groups will drift apart.'

Education statistics still sketch a skewered society. TER scores in eastern and northern suburbs are twice those in the south-west, and there are many more private schools, selective schools and universities in the east. University qualifications in the west are a third of those in the east, which reflects both the lower university intake of western students and also the perennial shift of university-educated western people to the city.

Where wealth goes, health follows. The west has more smokers and dangerous sun exposure and almost double the share of obese people. It therefore has a greater incidence of coronary heart disease. With its young population, it also has more car and pedestrian accidents. Not only are there more rich in the east and more poor in the west but there is a much greater demarcation between the two neighbourhoods. Fifteen years ago, a privileged Woollahra child might play next to a poor Surry Hills child in a park; a disadvantaged Balmain youth might go to school with a Hunters Hill boy. Today 50 kilometres of road separates most of them.

The inner-city poor were first ousted by the wave of young and educated people two decades ago. The second wave of gentrification is bringing millionaires into these traditional low-income areas. Professor Ian Burnley of the University of NSW's Geography Department says: 'The latest redevelopments in the inner east and inner west are mostly of a high standard; there are Balmain apartments starting at $1

million, and this will further concentrate the population of wealthy in the city.'

As the east loses its poorer suburbs and the west loses its status suburbs, the cultural divide is bound to deepen. Interaction between the two areas is also petering out. If the eastern elite view the west only through windscreens on their way to the snow, the west is less inclined to come to the city.

The only resource with which the west is well endowed, shopping malls, means western residents no longer have to come to the city to shop. The outskirts are now closer to Wollongong beaches (via roads) than city beaches and fewer are coming into the city for entertainment. Darling Harbour, which was touted as the entertainment centre for western Sydney (no doubt because it is on the western edge of the CBD) attracts only one in six of its visitors from the west.

Says Raskall: 'If you are not in contact with people from other classes, how does this affect your attitude? What attitudes are kids going to have when they have grown up with no contact with other classes? The us-versus-them ethos might be a short-term response; long-term it may develop into a great divide in the cultures.'

The division of Sydney is a challenge to social stability. The idea that Sydney's entree into the club of international cities will be accompanied by the employment ghettos and social stratifications that have bedevilled other world cities should be of concern to governments.

But it isn't. The lawyer John Mant, who recently completed a report on urban strategies for the NSW Government, is amazed at the lack of government concern and the pervasive ignorance of the west.

Mant says he 'routinely' found

ignorance of the west in government departments and this, he said, was infusing government policy with an eastern paradigm. 'In most cities,' he says, 'decision-makers can live in a number of geographic areas. In Sydney they live above the 240-foot contour or on the water. You can draw lines around those areas and capture just about all the decision makers.'

The geographic disadvantage of the west, Mant says, has been exacerbated by economic changes 'so the east increasingly looks outward to the world and is part of the international economy whereas the west belongs to the Australian economy and competes with places like Geelong, western suburbs of Melbourne and Adelaide'.

The west has been underprivileged since the postwar generation began pushing out the limits of the city in the quest for a quarter-acre block and an affordable house. The newness of the suburbs meant services always lagged behind suburb formation but there was a presumption that eventually services would follow. Some services did follow the population—shops, clubs, sports—but many, private and public, failed to show up in the west, and those that did showed up in much more modest shares than are enjoyed by the east.

Initially there was a certain homogeneity to the residents of the west—mostly Australian, young families with small children, working class to middle class, trades-educated. With limited access to culture and city diversions, the west developed its own lifestyles and its own attitudes. In particular, people living there began to think of themselves as the 'them' in the 'us-and-them'.

'There is a mystique about the west. It's seen as being different ▶

and if you're not living there (and most decision-makers don't live there) you don't know any better,' says Dave McCaughan, who used to conduct bus tours of the west for McCann-Erickson's clients before he moved to Asia. That an advertising agency saw a need to conduct tours of the west for corporate decision-makers spoke eloquently of the city-slickers' ignorance.

Since it first defended its 'westie' image, the west has changed. No longer white, male, Anglo country, it has great populations of immigrants, more single parent households than before (but no more than average) and, a sense of place that keeps some of its home-grown elite in the west. Significantly, says McCaughan, some of the west's millionaires, Tony Perich, Frank Oliveri and others are now prepared to boast publicly of their commitment to the west.

Most importantly, it now has a history.

'A lot of people live here because they choose to, not because they have to,' says McCaughan. 'Now it's a place where they grew up and where they want their own children to grow up.

'The west has developed its own culture, built around the pub culture and the shopping-centre culture; it also has its own approach to life, the people share common expectations and outlooks. What hasn't changed is the east's attitude to the west. It's only in the western sub-urbs that you are asked to justify why you live there.'

The east has changed, too. Richer, more multicultural, greater high-density living, fewer children, more educated and, as Mant pointed out, an international perspective that prompts the city to look to the world for its cues. But it's likely that the east's attitude to the west has changed, too. The term 'westie' is more often heard in the west today—even on the lips of a professor of surgery—than in the east. Is the east less antagonistic towards the west? Or is the east simply less interested? With the allure of the global marketplace and Asian business opportunities, it is likely that the east's antagonism to the west has turned to indifference.

Unemployment

East (except inner city and airport area), 6% or less. West ranges from 6% to 26%.

No qualifications

In most of the east, 50% are unqualified. In most of the west, 68% are unqualified.

Trade qualification

Less than 10% in most of the east. More than 16% in most of the west.

Education

HSC students average a TER of 70–84 in the east. In the west, average TER 30–40 . . .

Disease

In the east, greater incidence of AIDS, syphilis and hepatitis A. In the west, greater incidence of hepatitis B, salmonella and rubella.

University qualification

More than 18% in most of the east. Less than 6% in the west.

High-income earners

More than 12% in east. Less than 3% in west (except Georges River).

Managers and administrators

15% or more in most of the east; 6% or less in most of the west.

Health risk factors

Obesity—east 6%–7%, west 10%–11%.
Rarely or never apply sun protection—east 20%–32%, west 34%–43%.
Smokers—east 13%–18%, west 21%–22%.

Coronary heart disease mortality

Significantly higher in the west.

Lung cancer incidence and mortality

Significantly higher in the west.

Motor vehicle and pedestrian accidents

Significantly higher than State average in west. Significantly lower in east.

Source: ABS, the NSW Health Report, NSW Department of Education.

Sydney Morning Herald
5 October 1996

Questions

1. Deirdre Macken identifies increasing inequality between Sydney's east and west. What are the main inequalities that she points to?

2. What do the terms gentrification and social polarisation mean? Why is it occurring in Sydney? To what extent does this explain social processes occurring in the area you live in?

3. Macken argues that interaction between poor and affluent neighbourhoods of Sydney is 'petering out'. What evidence does she offer for this trend? Is this development of 'two worlds' characteristic of Australian society as a whole?

4. Macken cites national employment statistics indicating that male employment rates have fallen twice as fast in poorer neighbourhoods than in affluent ones, and that while women's employment rates have increased in affluent neighbourhoods, they have fallen 40 per cent in the poorest neighbourhoods. What might the social consequences of these changes be?

5. Macken argues 'where the wealth goes, health follows'. What are the sociological explanations for this observation? Which explanation is the most convincing?

6. An advertising agent interviewed in the article recounts that he used to conduct bus tours around poorer areas for corporate decision makers. What does this suggest about power structures in Australian society?

7. Explain the argument that the east of Sydney is part of the international economy, whereas the west is part of the national economy?

8. Macken argues that the east's antagonism to the west has turned to indifference. Why does she argue this? To what extent does this reflect broader social patterns in Australian society?

9. Should this east–west conflict be analysed in terms of class? Which sociological approach to class is most helpful in the analysis of this situation?

OVER TO YOU

Design a project to explore some of the main themes presented in this article. Your university library should have ABS Community Profile data, available by postcode. Compare two suburbs in your city. Who would you need to interview to explore issues raised in this article? What types of experiences could you attempt to understand? What sorts of sociological frameworks would be useful to structure your work around? Undertake exploratory interviews, and present the results to your tutorial. Deirdre Macken argues that eventually we may all pay for the burdens of this great divide. Is she right?

▇2▇ Class consciousness

Blue collar blues—addressing the state of the unions

By MICHAEL LYNCH

Want to get cheap loans without having to worry about the pitfalls in the small print? Need a discount on your health insurance? Interested in reductions on consumer durables, furniture, even food, through a bulk-buying scheme?

Perhaps a 50 per cent saving on a masters degree is more your line? Or a cut-price fee from your share-broker as he executes a transaction to reweight your portfolio? If you thought this type of pitch came from private sector businesses desperate to attract new customers you would be wrong. Deals like these —and they are only a few of the options on offer—are being made by trade unions Australia-wide as they struggle to rebuild their battered membership rolls. Union membership has been in decline since at least the early 1980s. Unions no longer capture the interest of the country's workforce as they once did.

With a hostile Government in Canberra, union officials such as ACTU assistant secretary Mr Bill Mansfield cannot ignore the figures which show membership has plunged from 49.5 per cent of workers in 1982 to 35 per cent in 1994, according to ABS figures.

'We have had a decline for a significant number of years.

We have not been growing our membership numbers alongside the growing number of workers, so the decline has been absolute,' he admits.

The ACTU itself has established a financial services operation to

provide advice, loans and broker cheaper financial services deals for its members. And while Mr Mansfield says such initiatives by the peak body and individual unions have 'been useful . . . they have not been sufficient'.

'Some of the things have been very popular. The union shopper scheme in Queensland, an organisation where union members can ring up to order an item and the buyers, professionals who know where all the outlets are, will get the cheapest price for them, has worked well and may be extended down the east coast. We are also currently negotiating a five per cent discount on all holiday packages with Ansett through its Traveland division.

'But we have got to look at the day-to-day industrial services that unions provide to members, the assistance to unions in organisations, in workplaces, what sort of advice we provide about negotiations. Without good quality services at that ground level we won't be saved.'

Those views are endorsed by Julie Venamore and Lynn Ridge, respectively assistant general secretary and educational and marketing officer with the NSW Nurses Association. Their union has reversed the downward membership spiral, its number of financial members having increased from 28,000 in 1986 to 44,000 today.

'We spend a lot of time and resources simply servicing our members and have taken several initiatives to help support branches

to make them more self-sufficient,' Ms Ridge says.

'The most important thing is that unions, just like any other business, have to be customer focused. They must stay relevant to the needs of their membership, otherwise they have got major problems. We have to keep members informed, help with grievances, handle a whole host of complaints, legal, financial and industrial,' says Ms Venamore.

Mr John Vines, executive director of the Association of Professional Engineers, Scientists and Managers, Australia (APESMA), says that while unions should never lose sight of their core responsibilities, they have to meet a changing marketplace by offering a range of broader services, something he believes has played a key role in APESMA's membership growth over the past few years.

APESMA currently runs an MBA in engineering management in conjunction with Deakin University. Course fees are $5000 for union members, $7500 for non-members, and some 50 per cent of students are APESMA members.

The union has an insurance company that offers cheap policies (including professional indemnity insurance) and also has a company called Engineering Placements, which is a recruiting agency for engineers. It recently established ties with a law firm, and its publications division produces regular remuneration surveys for engineers, industrial chemists, computer professionals and scientists.

Its latest move was to tie up a stockbroking service with ▶

stockbroking firm D & D Tolhurst Ltd, which offers members discount on broking and advisory fees—something which will doubtless be a popular service with the 35 per cent of APESMA members who own shares. 'We have to develop services much more geared for the individual.

'Unions have to offer industrial advice, but also recognise that at the end of the day they are in the business of customer service. Services can attract and help retain members.'

Sunday Age
18 August 1996

Questions

1. What does *class consciousness* mean? Why might levels of unionisation be an indicator of class consciousness?

2. Traditionally, unions appealed to members on the basis of a shared *identity* as workers—an identity based on common work experience, local cultures, and shared destiny. Modern union organisations are addressing potential members as consumers, not workers. Why?

3. Will unions become 'just like any other business'? What does this model imply in terms of unions representing a social group or social class?

4. The model of the *welfare state* which emerged in industrial societies this century was in part driven by the hopes of the labour movement for a new and fairer society. What does it mean for political culture when 'customer focus' replaces 'the light on the hill'?

OVER TO YOU

Interview two groups of people, one made up of union members, and one that is not. What are their reasons for joining or not joining unions? To what extent are questions of class consciousness present? Are these decisions made on the basis of worker identity, local or family tradition, or consumer identity?

3 Health and society

Hospital blunders under fire

By IAN VERRENDER

Patients and the community are bearing the cost of hundreds of thousands of avoidable mistakes by doctors and health workers in Australian hospitals every year, a landmark investigation has found.

Of an estimated 400,000 operations and medical procedures that go wrong each year—ranging from infections to death—230,000 could have been prevented, the report of the Federal Department of Human Services and Health Professional Indemnity Review reveals.

And while half of these left patients with a serious disability, fewer than 2,000 negligence claims against doctors and health workers were lodged each year, and 'only a handful of cases where liability is disputed go to court'.

The majority of these appeared to be won by the health profession, the report found. As a result, it concludes, the vast bulk of the costs of medical negligence are borne by the community, the victims of negligence, and their families.

'For example, lost income is met through sick leave, social security and, in some cases, simply doing without,' it said. 'The services required and costs relating to disability are met through a broad range of community services.'

Sydney Morning Herald
18 March 1996

Alternative therapy—a new age of healing

By MELISSA SWEET

You name it, Stephania Taylor has tried it. Since chronic fatigue syndrome (CFS) struck her in 1990, Taylor has spent tens of thousands of dollars on dozens of alternative therapies. First came chelation therapy—ridding the body of metals by putting chelating agents into the bloodstream, then high doses of intravenous vitamin C, ozone therapy (in which blood was drained from her body, pumped with oxygen and then replaced), naturopathy, Chinese medicine, meditation, chiropractic and homeopathy.

None brought lasting improvement, but Taylor, 37, and her husband, Stephen, persisted in their search because mainstream medicine had little to offer in the way of explanations or treatments for CFS.

By 1993, when she spent most of the year in bed, she had even tried spiritual healing, in which her aura was massaged. Then she bought kittens, 'which actually made a big difference', and read about laughing therapy. In the next six months, she watched about 600 videos, which made her laugh a lot—but didn't get rid of the CFS.

'It helped keep my attitude positive and it helped keep my willpower to live which was very faltering at that time,' she recalled, sitting in her sunny Balgowlah flat.

By this time she was quite a connoisseur of the alternative scene. She saw how therapists tended to blame her when their treatments made no difference. 'There was the implication it was my fault, that I wasn't co-operating, that I didn't want to get well,' she says.

'Getting the toxins out is a familiar phrase around alternative medicine. It's an easy explanation of negative results. You have to get worse before you get better.' In desperation and depression, Taylor and her husband contemplated trying a clinic in the Dominican Republic but decided the $25,000 cost involved was too much of a risk.

Then a friend sent a flyer promoting a Korean healing, called Chun Do Sun Bup Ki—energy treatment, which claimed to cure everything from infertility to high blood pressure and migraine. They were suspicious and weary, but attended a free lecture one Wednesday night in April this year, which introduced them to Ki's singing, chanting, meditation and slow movements.

'Three weeks later she was running up the steps in front of me,' Stephen said. 'Six weeks later she drove over to the centre herself.' Taylor is convinced the therapy has cured her.

Stephen, who now attends Ki classes with his wife, remains sceptical about the theory behind the technique—that it balances energy flows—but says he has been convinced by his wife's recovery and wants to publicise their story. ▶

'We have got our life back out of this,' he says.

Whether the treatment would help other people with CFS is questionable, according to the ME/Chronic Fatigue Syndrome Society of NSW. The society has no formal policy on alternative therapies, which it says are tried by most people with CFS.

'Some things might help one person, but they might make the next person worse,' says Patricia Murphy, just retired as the society's president. Murphy believes she is on the verge of recovery after battling the illness for the past several years, during which time she tried some alternative therapies. But she cannot be sure whether any made a difference, or whether she would have recovered anyway.

Dr Rob Loblay, a clinical immunologist at the Royal Prince Alfred Hospital, has seen many patients who claim to have been helped by therapies—ranging from ice-cold baths to colonic irrigation—but says it is usually difficult to evaluate their effect.

He is not surprised that people who modify their diet as part of a naturopathic regime often report improvement, as a significant proportion of CFS patients have food intolerance. Other patients recover spontaneously, while some perceive themselves to be better although their condition has not really changed. Dr Loblay is concerned about the lack of regulation of alternative therapies and notes that many CFS patients suffer adverse reactions to herbal therapies. He has also seen many patients go into enormous debt to pursue hopes which do not eventuate.

'There's no one thing that is going to fix everybody,' he says. 'If they are lucky enough to hit on something by chance which makes them feel better, and it's not doing any harm, then that is probably OK.'

Sydney Morning Herald
13 September 1995

Questions

1. How typical is Stephania Taylor? What does her experience illustrate about changing conditions of health and illness?

2. Modern medicine was once a paradigm of Weberian *rationalisation* and *secularisation*. Does the current rapid expansion of alternative therapies point to a crisis of this model?

3. Do such therapies point to a return of magic in Western culture, or at least to the end of a long process of secularisation that *Weber* believed was central to modernity?

4. To what extent can this experience be interpreted in terms of people's attempts to take control of their own health experiences? Does this point to the end of the *sick role* as defined by Talcott Parsons?

Pressured GPs say they are tempted to quit

By STEVE DOW

Half of all general practitioners are so stressed they have considered quitting, a national survey has found.

About three-quarters of the 320 metropolitan GPs studied also felt their stress was either constant or getting worse. General practitioners were also loath to seek professional help. While they generally reported talking to family and friends, they frequently kept problems bottled up.

'It's part of the denial by GPs (when) they can't cope,' said Dr Peter Schattner, the director of research at Monash University's department of community medicine and general practice, who co-wrote the study with a psychologist, Mr Greg Coman, last year.

The threat of litigation was their biggest fear, but the more frequent causes of stress included pressure to see patients, paperwork, phone interruptions, intrusion of work on family life, inadequate earnings, pressure to bulk bill, home visits and unrealistic community expectations.

Dr Schattner said the results reflected the need to overhaul the remuneration to doctors under Medicare. Rebates had failed to keep pace with inflation over the past few years.

'Doctors need to feel they are being rewarded for the effort they put in,' Dr Schattner said. 'To expect GPs to continue to provide the same level of service but to ▶

decrease their incomes is either asking GPs to drop their standards or get increasingly stressed as they try to maintain their standards.'

The study, funded by the Federal Government's general practitioner evaluation program, appears to conflict with a recent British study, which found GPs were less stressed if they were busier.

But Dr Schattner said the British study might reflect doctors who practised more 'superficial medicine' — similar to doctors in Australia who worked for big bulk-billing clinics — but GPs in their own practices had a greater sense of commitment to their work.

The Age
12 February 1997

Breast cancer test privatised

By MELISSA SWEET

A United States Nobel Prize winner is set to launch the world's first commercial genetic test for a common cancer, costing women up to $US1,000 ($1,298) if they have it done on the breast cancer gene that he 'owns'.

Professor Walter Gilbert expects his company to receive the patent for BRCA1, the first identified breast cancer gene, next year, and says the commercial test to detect cancer-causing mutations on the gene will be launched this year.

But its introduction is expected to raise major ethical, medical and financial dilemmas.

The multi-millionaire scientific entrepreneur and 1980 Nobel Prize winner for chemistry has horrified Australian experts by suggesting that women who have breast cancer, and especially those with a history of the disease, should be tested.

In the longer term, he expects women with any family history of the cancer, and eventually all women, to be tested.

Professor Gilbert, who is co-founder of the biotechnology company Myriad Genetics, and holds a professorship at Harvard University, said Australian doctors would be able to mail DNA samples to his company in Salt Lake City for BRCA1 mutation testing.

Each test was expected to cost about $US1,000, although he expected this would drop as it became more widely used.

Myriad expects to receive the patent on BRCA1 next year, after winning the race to identify it in 1994, and has also applied to patent another breast cancer gene, BRCA2, for which Professor Gilbert expects a commercial test will be launched next year.

The professor says 85 per cent of women with BRCA1 mutations would develop breast cancer, and 50 per cent would develop ovarian cancer.

But leading cancer geneticists, who met at the National Breast Cancer Centre (NBCC) in Sydney last week to develop guidelines for breast cancer genetic screening, said these comments were irresponsible, and suggested that Professor Gilbert may be motivated by commercial considerations.

They said the tests should be offered only to carefully selected women through clinics able to give counselling and support, and warned that there was no proven way of preventing cancer in women at increased genetic risk.

'The potential of (testing) doing harm is enormous and the potential for doing good is only very small,' said Dr Sally Redman, director of the NBCC.

Dr John Hopper, head of genetic epidemiology at the University of Melbourne, said much more work was needed to determine the test's accuracy before it was widely used.

Sydney Morning Herald
25 March 1996

Next up — one-step medical care

By MARION DOWNEY

'It's convenient for the customer and efficient for the business' — Health Care Revolution.

The company that set up the country's first privately run public hospital in 1994, Port Macquarie Base, has been buying radiology, pathology and general practices in NSW and other States to provide consumers with 'one-stop' health care. ▶

Healthcare of Australia is the nation's largest hospital operator, with 36 private hospitals and two privately run public hospitals. 'If you go into a travel agent they can arrange everything for you—hotels, flights, insurance, car hire,' the managing director of Healthcare of Australia, Dr Barry Catchlove, said. 'It's convenient for the customer and efficient for the business. There's no reason why health care cannot be the same.' The latest arrival on the Australian health scene, the American $23 billion health care provider Columbia/HCA, is planning to offer a similar service. Its chief executive, Mr Geoff Sam, said he also intends to move into one-stop 'seamless health care' offering everything from hospital places to pathology, radiology, and general practice . . .

In its annual report, Healthcare calls the policy 'value-adding through vertical integration'. Last December, Dr Catchlove tried to reassure doctors working for or contracted to Healthcare.

The company has faced accusations, he wrote, that 'by ownership of private hospitals, pathology and medical centres, we can force patterns of practice on clinicians involved in our organisations'.

But, he said, it was not in doctors' contracts that they had to use Healthcare's facilities, 'even though it is true we would like them to do so'. Dr Catchlove said this week: 'There is a lot of hype and nonsense talked about these things.

'The relationship is between the doctor who organises the tests; it is between the pathologist and the GP. Successful practices depend on building that relationship, in truth, getting more efficient, better organised and bigger.'

In any case, Dr Catchlove said, the company was responding to an agenda, not setting one.

'We don't make the rules. We are not trying to set the agenda.'

Sydney Morning Herald
15 February 1997

Study finds men live longer in east

By DARREN GRAY

Men in Melbourne's western suburbs have a premature death rate 43 per cent higher than in the east, according to the latest State Government health audit.

The report, which records the key health measures for all metropolitan regions, shows that in 1994 the rate of male deaths under the age of 75 in the west was 469.4 per 100,000, compared with 328.3 in the eastern suburbs.

The figures show residents of the eastern suburbs go to hospital least often, have the lowest mortality rate and the lowest death rate from heart attack of all Melburnians.

The western suburbs have the highest rate of hospital visits and the second-highest mortality rate, behind the northern suburbs.

The report, 'Health Indicators', shows that while the western suburbs scored worst in some areas, the region did best in others.

It had the lowest infant death rate, the lowest rate of death among women from stroke and the lowest death rate among women from cancer.

By slim margins, the northern suburbs had the highest male death rate from strokes in 1994 and the lowest proportion of children starting school with completed immunisation certificates.

While the health census shows some disparities between suburbs, overall there are strong indications that our health is improving. For both men and women, deaths from heart disease and stroke have fallen significantly over the past two decades.

'Health Indicators' also shows that lung cancer death rates for men have fallen slightly over the past 20 years, while for women they have risen.

Suicide rates for young men have steadily risen but for women the rate has been fairly static.

Dr Peter Schattner, the director of research at Monash University's department of community medicine and general practice, said that it was no surprise that men in the western suburbs had the highest premature death rate and the second-highest heart disease death rate.

'It is a fact of life that if you are wealthier and have a more yuppie lifestyle the chances are that you will be healthier and less likely to have a heart attack,' he said.

The Health Minister, Mr Rob Knowles, said more needed to be done to reduce the incidence of smoking among blue collar workers.

Source: Department of Human Services (Health Indicators report).

Sunday Age
16 February 1997

If age persists

By HELEN HAWKES

In Hollywood's fountain of youth fable, Cocoon, a decrepit group of senior citizens are miraculously rejuvenated when they frolic in water inhabited by gigantic alien shells. Absurd though it may have been, the film was a huge success, tapping as it did into the universal and eternal longing for a way to hold back the hands of time.

But where once the processes of ageing were considered inevitable, researchers and pharmaceutical companies claim recent discoveries are making it possible for them to replicate some of the body's own youth substances, opening the way to preventing—or even reversing—ageing.

Swiss Caps, the world's third-largest manufacturer of natural supplements, each week at its Zurich factory produces 40 million capsules, among them 'anti-agers' such as melatonin and gingko biloba.

Typical of the new, high-tech natural medicine being manufactured by the company is Zinax, a standardised ginger extract claimed to fulfil one part of the longevity promise: relief from a disease often associated with ageing, arthritis.

While Swiss Caps is making a healthy profit from these anti-agers, drug companies are working on their own versions to tap into the lucrative market.

The darling of the anti-ageing set is melatonin, dubbed 'the hottest pill of the decade' by *Newsweek* magazine in the US, and a plethora of books have been published to cash in on this anti-ageing fad.

Scientists now think that the genes involved in ageing are controlled by hormones that act as chemical messengers to the genes.

When the hormones get depleted, ageing sets in.

Melatonin is made in the brain's pineal gland and in almost all animal species studies, its presence is an indication that it is night-time. It is produced during the hours of darkness from the body's master clock, the suprachiasmatic nuclei or SCN, then switched off by morning light.

In the battle for lifelong health. Melatonin is 'top dog', says research scientist Michael Colgan, director of the Colgan Institute of Nutritional Science and author of *Hormonal Health*.

The decline of melatonin in old age is so reliable, says Colgan, that researchers at the New York Academy of Sciences now refer to the pineal gland as the Ageing Clock. 'A mass of studies by neuro-endocrinologists points to melatonin deficit being connected with an increased risk of cancer, cardiovascular disease, senility and a host of other diseases, he says.

Where Colgan advocates supplementing melatonin levels orally—he takes 3 mg every night—Professor Ray Kearney, head of the University of Sydney's department of infectious diseases, says it may be more sound in the long term to undertake lifestyle changes, in eating and exercise, to boost melatonin to youthful levels. He warns that taking too much melatonin can aggravate underlying auto-immunity diseases such as arthritis.

Another hormonal substance at the forefront of new longevity claims is dehydroepiandrosterone or DHEA—the major circulating adrenal hormone in the body. In 1994, Roussel Uclaf, the man behind the French abortion pill RU486, said he believed DHEA was a cure for ageing. DHEA is the most abundant steroid hormone in our bodies, secreted by the adrenal glands and then converted into customised hormones used almost everywhere: in the testes and the ovaries, in placentas, foetuses, lungs, skin and brain.

Recently William Regelson, American microbiologist and oncologist and author of the *Melatonin Miracle*, released a book entitled *The Superhormone Promise*, in which he added to the DHEA mystique by claiming that the substance 'restores energy, improves mood, increases sex drive, enhances memory, relieves stress, reduces body fat and even makes your skin softer and your hair shinier'.

But Stephen Twigg, endocrine fellow at the Royal North Shore Hospital, warns potential users to be cautious of taking the substance for anti-ageing reasons, citing suggestions of increased risk of cancer and liver toxicity.

Anti-agers say another substance, DMAE—dimenthylaminoethanol—may also play a part in longevity by boosting the levels of the neurotransmitter acetylcholine, and thus enhancing cognitive function.

So too, it is claimed, can the leaf extract gingko biloba, which works by dilating blood vessels.

In Australia many people are experimenting with substances such as melatonin, although, unlike Americans, most prefer not to broadcast it.

Good Weekend
Sydney Morning Herald & *The Age*
3 May 1997

Questions

1. Medicine was once seen as the model *profession*. What do sociologists mean by profession? To what extent do the high levels of dissatisfaction experienced by GPs point to a decline in the older model of professional autonomy?

2. Sociologists argue that we are witnessing the *medicalisation* of increasing areas of human experience. What does this term mean? To what extent is growing old being redefined as an illness? What are the likely social implications?

3. The rise of the medical profession was associated with the rise of the *biomedical model* of health—the expansion of the welfare state and its health programs, and cultural deference given to professionals. Increasingly, all three of these factors are being contested. Examine each of the articles in this section. Are they representative of significant change?

4. Melissa Sweet reports that a company 'owns' the first identified breast cancer gene. What are the implications of the market model present here?

5. The development of 'one-stop' medical care points to a shift in medicine, from a 'client–professional' to a 'customer–business' relationship. What are the potential implications of this change?

6. Darren Gray reports that rates of premature death are 43 per cent higher in Melbourne's working-class suburbs as compared with middle-class suburbs. What are the sociological explanations for this pattern, and which of these is the most convincing? Are the shifts to market models likely to change this?

7. In pre-industrial society disease took the form of social catastrophe, where up to 25 per cent of a society's population could be wiped out. With the emergence of industrial society, the nature of disease changed—from the social catastrophe associated with infectious disease, to the individual problems associated with the degenerative and cardio-vascular diseases. Are we witnessing a change yet again, with an emerging imperative of health and the increased medicalisation of experiences such as classroom inattention and ageing?

OVER TO YOU

Interview a group of people about their experience of health and illness and if possible explore experiences associated with the 'patient', 'customer', 'medicalised' and 'alternative' models of health. To what extent do these interviews reveal different models of the meaning of health? What social actors do respondents talk about (e.g. bureaucrats, technology corporations, alternative therapists, professionals, community-based groups and social movements)? What social models of illness and healthiness do your interviews reveal? Do these point to the power of different social actors, such as corporations or professionals, to shape what it means to be healthy? Can we analyse models of health in terms of models of the relationship between self-identity and society, and to what extent do your interviews point to health as a 'contested' social experience?

4 Social inequality—education

The education divide

By JANET McCALMAN

It will be a painful year for education. The Vanstone cuts are under way and dreadful things are happening around the country. Education in this country is at a turning point.

But in all the debate about cuts to all levels of education, few will talk about the real issues at stake—the decline in the knowledge base of Australian children and the effect this is having on university learning as well as on the young people struggling to find employment.

In 1996 for the first time in Victoria the Minister for Education released the final school year (VCE) results for the top 7.5 per cent of students. They were listed by name, by school, even by school type. State school can be compared with private school, Catholic with Protestant.

These results are nothing less than a political scandal. They expose an education system poisoned by unfairness and low achievement, a system that will condemn us to severe cultural and economic decline in the next millennium.

The 1996 VCE results reveal whole swathes of Melbourne and rural Victoria where even the able are being robbed of their right to a good education. Let's look at compulsory English, the measure of literacy and competence. Thirty-three 'classic' western suburbs government schools produced fewer high achievers in English than University High School, which draws more than half its students from low-income families.

With University High added to the total, plus the handful of 'middle-class' high schools in the northern suburbs, the entire government system north of the Yarra still did little better than just the Methodist Ladies College. Even in English as a second language, private schools and middle-class high schools outperformed the western and northern suburbs. It is not possible for there to be so few able young people in that vast population north of the Yarra.

In mathematical methods, the 'middle range' subject where you might expect linguistically deprived immigrant children or working-class bright students to shine, these 33 schools did one third as well as University High. In specialist mathematics, the result was half, as it was in physics. There were no high achievers at all in either literature or European history, for these subjects are rarely taught north of the Yarra. High achievement for the western suburbs, when it comes, is confined to the less academic side of the curriculum and to community languages.

Richard Teese, Associate Professor in Education at Melbourne University, has been showing that failure rates in English in the VCE are actually rising in the western suburbs. It has been the middle class that has come out the winners from a system, he argues, that we designed to benefit 'a highly organised, middle-class model learner'. In fact, an achievement table needs to be added for all the parents who did their children's project-based research, corrected and even wrote the drafts. Privately, teachers everywhere confess to grave fears about whether students are doing the work themselves.

So the poor are double losers. Not only have their needs been neglected, they are competing against privileged people who have the money and the gall to bend the rules.

For all the talk of excellence from the Government and the successful, the other scandal is that our children are learning less than they did a generation ago.

The reasons for the inequalities of our system run deeper than resources and staffing. Neither can we blame the teachers; quite the reverse. There are more than enough men and women able to teach in this state, although many have left the profession, exhausted and disillusioned. But they are there in the community if we had the will to turn our education system around tomorrow.

However we can blame curriculum planners and policy-makers and academics and politicians of both sides, for the decline even started before the economic rationalists came to power. Australian education became beguiled by the romance of the democratic curriculum. Knowledge that was structured and systematised was implicated with authoritarianism. Children should direct their own learning, be free and creative, for lessons learnt by discovery are those that are learnt best.

The teacher's task was to train students in process (i.e. method); content (i.e. knowledge) was a byproduct. Learning was thus trivialised. All our schools claim they are offering 'quality education' but only about 10 per cent of schools are teaching the hard academic ▶

subject seriously and with success. And those schools, with the addition of a few new faces, are really the same that were doing so in the 1930s.

University staff from all over Australia are now complaining of serious deficiencies in basic knowledge in the humanities, mathematics and the sciences. Too many university students are functionally illiterate, culturally illiterate and unable to reckon. They can think for themselves, but they don't know enough . . .

Contrary to intentions, the progressive educational reforms of the 1980s appear to have reduced the capacity of even the highest-scoring university students for independent learning. They expect their university teachers to read their drafts and discuss their essays and direct their reading just as happened at school.

A Monash University colleague was confronted by a young woman who complained that she 'normally scored As and he was giving her only Cs.'

'But that's what your work deserved.'

'Well, it's your fault—it's up to you to make sure I get As,' she replied.

The truth must come out: the emperor has no clothes and our children are getting robbed. The greatest danger to our lucrative overseas student market is not racism but the falling academic standards of our secondary school system and undergraduate courses.

But worst of all, unless we invest in our most important natural resource of all, the intellectual capital of our people, we will become a backward, poor, crime-ridden, divided and unhappy nation. We are squandering the talents of our people.

Much of our progress since the Second World War has come from the expansion of secondary and tertiary education and the infusion of talent and energy from migration. We are now losing that. Our young brightest and best are interested in money and power, not in becoming scientists and teachers and thinkers. And our poor are doomed to remain on the outside, always looking in.

The Age
20 January 1997

Questions

1. Janet McCalman suggests that 'progressive education' models which emphasise students' autonomy and ability to organise themselves in project-based learning, may in fact advantage middle-class students more than working-class students. Why might this be so?

2. Failure rates in the only compulsory final year subject, English, are rising in working-class suburbs. What sociological explanations could be advanced to explain this? Which is the most convincing?

3. Education is increasingly being restructured along free market lines with a number of Australian universities now referring to their students as 'customers'. This suggests that students are economically rational actors. Is this all there is to education?

4. Schools were once seen as a vehicle of social justice and reform. During the 1980s governments increasingly defined education in terms of economic benefits. It is increasingly argued that educational inequalities ultimately reflect student ability, and those who fail are lazy or morally inadequate. Can this explanation account for the distribution of high results, where for example, in many disciplines there are no high achievers at all in working-class areas?

5. McCalman argues that the brightest students are interested in power and money, not in becoming teachers, scientists or thinkers. Is this the case, and if so, why? What are the implications of this argument for society as a whole?

OVER TO YOU

Interview two groups of young people—one at an 'elite' high school, the other at a working-class state high school. Ask them to talk about their educational experience, and the reasons for staying on at school or for leaving. What sociological frameworks best make sense of what you have learnt? Present your results to your tutorial group.

5 School experience

Classroom surprises for a fill-in teacher

By TIMOTHY RAWLINS

Timothy Rawlins is a relieving language teacher. He found life as a new teacher wasn't quite what he expected. His short text captures many of the decisive transformations of education.

One is first struck by the sense of being observed. The rumour is already about that I will be teaching here. 'Are you going to teach us?' one youth asks. 'Are you an undercover cop?' he continues, not waiting for the answer to the first question.

The second is one that will be frequently asked in the next week. They are not used to teachers in suits. 'Yes, I am an undercover cop.' How else to reply? The students are inquisitive but tactless, humorous but rude. There is a sense of general vulgarity.

There are also the students who embrace in the corridor.

Often both girls, but also girls and boys. Did we ever do that? It is very direct and kind, obviously a sign of friendship, perhaps a little too contrived. It is a little surprising, but also encouraging.

Sensitivity towards others, though, is not an operating concept for the great majority. And those who hug their friends can be among the most vitriolic at insulting and cursing those who cross them.

Personalities are often crude and abrupt, not always matched by the confidence to act. Despite all this, the students are generally kind— clumsy, but kind. They totally dominate the environment. The corridor is thick to the point almost of oppression with personalities. It does not smell good. It smells of school,

of body odour, of carpet that has had shoes walking on it for years.

The light is quite poor. Decoration is an afterthought. Paint is flaking. Devoid of people, it is quite barren. The students give it life, decorate it with their presence. Crowded, it is at least bearable and there is a sense, however chaotic, of an underlying purpose. Without them it is a disappointing location.

Many of the classrooms are too small for the classes, especially N4. Tables are too small, too narrow, too close together. There is no way for the teacher to easily circulate with three longitudinal rows of tables. Students at the front cannot see the opposite end of the board.

Students can easily find their gear spilling over on to their neighbours. It is easy to touch the books of neighbouring students, to take things from pencil cases, to push books on to the floor. All these forms of disruption occur frequently.

The room is crowded. This provides easy access for each student to the spaces of others. Studies by anthropologists tell us that certain cultures require more personal space than others.

In our culture, with the focus on individual expression, it definitely feels too crowded in there.

Of course, the teacher I was replacing had already warned me about the smallest rooms. The quality of the furniture is poor—these are the same style of chairs and tables that I studied on in the 1970s. There is some egalitarian philosophy involved perhaps, but the furniture seems patronisingly small and cheap. It is not suitable for a work environment.

The physical environment in general offers little to recommend itself as a place of learning. The school is too large, too crowded and too dependent on a particular form of timetable.

There is too much going on. Diversity of subjects makes for interesting reading at report time. So, 40 minutes here, 40 minutes there. We teach them many things. We keep them mobile. Motion becomes the theme. Perhaps this succeeds in maintaining interest.

If nothing else, the bored are always eventually saved by the bell, motion to a new location, a new scenario, perhaps something that more appeals to them, a teacher who better has their measure.

Even those who have already fallen away from the content of the program, semi-literate, innumerate, dreadfully disruptive in language other than English, continue the form of classes, and shadow the program at the same speed as those who have consumed it all and can keep up with the tempo.

The library has a computer catalogue and a colour machine set up with an interactive CD with an audio-visual encyclopedia. It looks flashy. The shelves, however, are relatively denuded. Many texts date back to the '70s, '60s or even '50s in the geographic and 'social history' section. It is possible that such dated books can no longer serve for geography or social history at all. Some of those forests they talk about aren't there any more.

There is, for the most part, a discourse of conservative propaganda and patronising texts targeted at the perceived needs of the young. It ▶

is nothing that we would read to further our understanding of life's mysteries and difficulties. There is nothing that adults could possibly get much from beyond facts and figures. There is nothing that really passes as philosophy, or theology, precious little which could pass for critical writing.

There are plenty of teenage story books. Perhaps that is what our youth need and relate to best. Perhaps it is not a deficiency that our actual cultural knowledge base— the sociology theory, philosophy, classics—are all conspicuously absent. It is a library, after all, of the recent history of Australian education. Very specialised. Students go there to socialise and some do work.

In the corridor—at the administrative rather than the teaching end—school trophies remind us of a distant time before the '70s when such things were valued. The school as a little nation, a model of competition, as a metaphor for the work.

The staffroom is a waystation for passing teachers. The majority are in their 40s and 50s and many of them are grey and visibly tired. One teacher speaks at once affectionately but accusingly of the students, as 'turkeys'. Perhaps things were better in the time of trophies.

Discourse focuses not on teaching and learning as viable, but at the frustration which is preventing it. 'X isn't working for me, is he working for you?' 'That T, I have never seen a boy who could make a smile offensive.'

For the newcomer, it is easy to implicate the veteran teachers for signs of failure. A few weeks of difficulty and failure change that. The teachers often talk of their difficulties as part of the process of overcoming them. After a week or so, the positive signs are clearer.

The dreaded 8C, who are often a rabble for the distraught French teacher, are a perfectly amiable, hard-working unit in art. Teachers are doing better or worse than myself. This is a remarkably cheerful discovery. Things can be better or worse. Neither failure nor success is truly a fixed thing.

On the vice-principal's desktop computer is a daily prayer. He is an avowed Christian, an almost unnaturally cheerful individual who is competent at the yelling, discipline, organisation and corridor-clearing that the job requires. There is both experience and support evident here. It is needed and appreciated.

The boss is a little inaccessible, not in terms of personality, but in terms of location, at the far end of the school, deep within the administrative complex. He is not in the centre of the school, which feels more to be the corridor before school and between classes. He is kind and competent. But what is his position? There is never a sense that this is a hierarchy, or that leadership is the guiding light of the system.

Discipline and curriculum are the task of the teachers. In six weeks of teaching, not once am I given directives on what to teach or how to conduct discipline. This is fine. As a professional, I cope. If there are any questions, I need only ask, and I do.

Sydney Morning Herald
4 June 1996

Questions

1. Sociologists have used the term *institution* to identify recurring forms of social organisation which involve *norms*, *roles* and *socialisation*. From Durkheim onwards, the school was seen as the clearest model of an institution. Give examples of the norms, roles and forms of socialisation that sociology has associated with the school as an institution.

2. If the school is a socialising institution, transmitting norms and values, the relationship between teacher and student is central to the educational experience. This appears still to be the case in primary school—but is it the case in secondary school? What do we learn about the teacher–student relationship from this article?

3. If we go into a workplace, we will encounter people acting in terms of roles and functions. What is striking in Timothy Rawlins' text is the power of a youth culture, much more shaped in terms of personality than a student culture produced by the school. Most new teachers are disconcerted when they encounter this youth culture, which seems totally independent of the school—it appears to them incomprehensible and aggressive. Is this the case here?

4. How can we explain the dominance of personality, and the weak sense of social role in the student culture?

5. Rawlins contrasts current school experience with 'a distant time before the 1970s', when the school was a 'little nation'; when school trophies held pride of place. This suggests an older educational model, based around norms, social *integration* and unifying *rituals*. What has happened to this 'little nation'?

6. The school appears to 'manage' students by 'keeping them mobile'. What sociological interpretations can we offer of this?

7. What does the school library tell us about the educational experience? The library is presented as a symbol of recent Australian education—one where sociology, philosophy and the classics are absent. Why?

8. What can we learn from Rawlins' article about what has replaced an educational experience once organised in terms of rituals, socialisation and norms? He argues that the school is not a hierarchy (as opposed to the 1960s where saluting the flag and marching into class were the norms). How can we describe the contemporary educational experience in sociological terms? Has a clear model emerged to replace the older model of school as an institution?

OVER TO YOU

Interview two groups of senior school students about their experiences of school. Define in advance what characterises an institution, and test—through your interviews—the extent to which the schools concerned are institutions. Present your conclusions, and the implications you draw from these, to your tutorial group.

From fordism to postfordism

The divided nation: Australia's work revolution

By STEPHEN LONG

Australia's workforce is divided: between the overworked and the out-of-work; between the well-paid and the poorly paid; between career jobs and fringe jobs.

The certainties of the postwar era—standard working hours, the dominance of full-time employment, a relative abundance of secure, middle-income jobs—have collapsed. Part-time, casual and contract work are replacing standard hours and standard roles. Jobs have moved en masse from manufacturing to services.

As organisations downsize—shedding labour in booms and busts—the very notion of 'permanent' employment has disappeared. Faced with global competition, business has pared back the workforce to a diminishing core of full-time jobs, supplemented by a growing periphery of casual and contract labour.

A two-tier labour market has emerged, polarised between high-wage earners and low-wage earners.

The implications for public policy are profound.

'Australia's labour market is more segmented, more divided than at any stage this century,' says John Buchanan, assistant director of the Australian Centre for Industrial Relations Research and Teaching (ACIRRT), and co-author of a report for the Brotherhood of St Laurence, Reforming Working Time. 'We now have the paradoxical situation of increasing hours of work for employed workers occurring simultaneously with rising levels of joblessness.'

The hard facts present a startling portrait of how work's basic characteristics are being redefined:

- The standard working week—38 hours worked over five days in predictable daytime hours—is no longer the dominant form of employment in Australia. Just over a third of the workforce now works 'standard' hours. It is affecting people's ability to plan their lives around predictable work. Australian Bureau of Statistics data on working time arrangements showed that last August, 36.5 per cent of the workforce had variable starting and finishing times. For two-thirds of these workers, the time they began and finished work varied each day.

- Large swathes of the workforce have been 'casualised', with one in four employees in Australia—24 per cent—now casual workers. By world standards, Australia's reliance on casual labour is extraordinary. It exceeds the level in all other OECD countries apart from Spain. Close to half a million employees are now full-time casual—almost 10 per cent of the full-time workforce. These workers are engaged in a precarious form of employment, lacking job security and, often, certainty in hours. Most have no access to 'community standard' employment conditions such as annual leave, sick leave and long-service leave.

- While joblessness grows, full-time employees are working longer and longer hours. Some 37 per cent of full-time employees worked an average of 49 or

more hours a week in February this year (up from 28 per cent a decade earlier), according to unpublished ABS data. Overall, the average working week for full-time employees has risen to 42.6 hours—up more than two hours a week on the figure 10 years ago—despite the supposed shift to a 38 hours-a-week norm in many industries. This is higher than anywhere in Europe, outside the UK. Managers and professionals have the highest incidence of very long working hours, but they are also common among plant operators and drivers, sales people, trades people and para-professionals.

- Almost a quarter of the workforce now works part-time, up from just 10 per cent 30 years ago. More than half the jobs created since the trough of the last recession, in mid-1991, have been part-time, and most of these new jobs are in low-paying sectors. According to Professor Bob Gregory of the Australian National University, 'virtually all of the jobs growth since the end of the 1970s, adjusted for population growth, is in part-time jobs'.

- In broad terms, there is an inverse relationship between employment growth and wage rates. In high-wage, high-skill industries, employment is falling. In the low-wage, low-skill industries, employment is rising.

- The number of people holding more than one job has almost doubled in the past 10 years, to more than 5 per cent of the labour force. To gain adequate income, 'people are having to ▶

quilt bits of jobs together', says Sue Jackson, director of the Brotherhood of St Laurence's Future of Work project.

- Almost 9 per cent of the workforce is officially unemployed and nearly 30 per cent of unemployed Australians—about 230,000 people—have been out of work for more than 12 months.
- The 'standard' working life—continuous employment from school leaving age to retirement—is a thing of the past. People are entering the workforce later and exiting earlier. Unemployment and childbirth are interrupting working lives. In 1966, some 59 per cent of male workers aged 15 to 19 held full-time jobs, compared with just 18 per cent today. Thirty years ago, almost 80 per cent of men aged between 60 and 65 were employed. Today, the percentage has almost halved, to 42 per cent. The teenage full-time job market has collapsed, while retrenchments and early retirement have seen the number of men employed until traditional retirement age plummet.

The transformation in the nature of work during the past decade has huge implications for many levels of public policy: industrial relations, education, child care, retirement policy, industry policy, even urban planning. Yet, extraordinarily, there has been little public debate on the issue in Australia, beyond a narrow focus on workplace reform.

Despite this, the gaps between policy and reality are manifest. Our welfare system and our entire superannuation structure are built on assumptions that grew out of the dominance of the male breadwinner working full-time for 40 years.

Unemployment provision, which was designed to provide short-term assistance to breadwinners, is struggling to cope with long-term unemployment and high rates of joblessness.

'The implications of the changes in work extend well beyond the confines of labour market policy,' says the eminent labour-market economist, Professor Bob Gregory. 'For example, what do you do about the fact that jobs are increasingly concentrated in one set of families and unemployment in another? What do you do about the divisions in the cities?'

The Brotherhood of St Laurence, one of the few groups to seriously examine the issue through its Future of Work project, says the transformation of the labour market may force a fundamental rethink of our whole approach to welfare.

'The tendency towards low-paid jobs or part-time or casual jobs, resulting in employment not yielding sufficient income for all labour-market participants, has broken down the employment/unemployment dichotomy,' according to its report, *Reading the Signs*. 'It is now possible for full-time employment, in a low-paid job, to yield less income than unemployment allowance in combination with rent assistance and some part-time earnings,' it said.

Already, the new labour market and competitive pressure have destroyed the postwar consensus built around full employment, universal welfare, and central wage fixing to dampen industrial conflict and protect the vulnerable. It has undermined traditional values such as egalitarianism and collectivism.

'Australian employees are hardening to the realities and disciplines of the global economy,' says John Stanek, the global head of Interna-

tional Survey Research, the world's largest collator of employee opinion surveys. 'All of the safety nets failed (protection, arbitration, unions) when the acid rain hit this part of the forest. It alienated Australian employees from unions, management and government. The only thing they could trust was themselves.'

In the 1990s, people's working-time preferences are more diverse than ever before. Multiple factors are fuelling this: women (and less often men) combining part-time work with family responsibilities; young people combining casual work with longer periods of formal education; an ageing population, with employment preferences changing over the life cycle. Social values and structures have changed, producing what German sociologist Karl Hinrichs calls 'an individualisation and diversification of people's experiences, situations and lifestyles'.

But the idea that there is a neat fit between changing employee preferences and employer's demands for greater flexibility is one of the big myths of the 1990s. The increase in part-time work and flexible hours has more to do with the needs of business than the desires of workers.

'It is possible, on occasions, for employer and employee interests on working hours to coincide,' says Iain Campbell of Monash University's National Key Centre for Industrial Relations, author of *The End of Standard Working Time?* 'But much of the flexibility employers are demanding is opposed to employees' preference for more individual control of their working time.'

In the past five years, employers have fought a highly successful campaign to make working hours ▶

more flexible to suit the requirements of their businesses, rolling back the gains of the union movements' 38-hour week campaign in the 1970s and 1980s.

According to John Buchanan, 'The push for flexible hours is primarily about fitting people into the requirements of production.'

Part-time work suits many employees, particularly women with families. But there is increasing evidence the rise in part-time work masks significant levels of underemployment.

In its 1995 Employment Outlook report, the OECD found Australia had the highest rates of 'involuntary' part-time employment among OECD nations. One in four part-time workers would like to work longer hours, ABS data shows. Quite simply, Australia is not creating enough full-time jobs to meet demand.

Indeed, the real unemployment rate would double to more than 16 per cent—and possibly soar to 22.3 per cent—if discouraged job-seekers and the underemployed were taken into account, according to a study by the National Institute of Labour Studies.

Welcome to the new world of work. The question is, how do we cope with its realities?

Australian Financial Review
23 September 1996

Questions

1. What were the certainties of the postwar era that Stephen Long talks about?

2. What does a 'two-tier' labour market mean?

3. What are 'standard hours', and what proportion of the workforce now work these hours?

4. In August 1996, 36.5 per cent of the Australian workforce had variable starting and finishing times. Combined with the decline of 'standard hours', what does this mean in terms of the extent to which social activities are 'synchronised' by work? What are implications of this change?

5. What do sociologists mean when they use the terms *fordism* and *postfordism*? To what extent can the changes Long describes be analysed in terms of a shift from 'fordism' to 'postfordism'?

6. Long argues that employees are alienated from unions, management and government, and the only thing they trust is themselves. Is there strong evidence to support this? Do societies need *trust*? Are there signs of a general decline of social trust, and what might this imply?

7. Sociologists point to a process of *individualisation* of experiences, or the *pluralisation* of lifestyles. Freedom, autonomy and authenticity have become more powerful cultural models than sameness and standardisation. But do the emerging models of work flexibility meet these cultural shifts? What is driving the reshaping of work?

8. Can we imagine other models of flexibility?

9. Long argues that there had been almost no political debate about the transformation of work and the new patterns emerging. What reasons could explain this? Do we need political debate in this area?

OVER TO YOU

Is there a shift in the relationship between economy and society as advanced by theories of postfordism? What are the main characteristics of postfordism? Can you explore these in terms of student work experiences? List the types of jobs that students in your tutorial have. What characterises these? Describe the work culture present. To what extent do these examples correspond to the postfordist model?

7 Rethinking work

Emerging new age calls for a new politics

By JEREMY RIFKIN

Thousands of jobs are being lost forever as economies are transformed by new technologies and companies embrace the ethos of downsizing. It's time, argues Jeremy Rifkin, for Australia to debate a shorter working week and to rethink traditional models of job creation.

The global economy is undergoing a fundamental transformation in the nature of work that will reshape civilisation in the 21st century. Sophisticated computers, teleommunications, robotics, and other Information Age technologies are fast replacing humans in virtually every sector and industry. Nowhere is the trend more evident than in Australia, where unemployment is close to 9 per cent.

The hard reality that economists and politicians are reluctant to acknowledge is that manufacturing and much of the service sector are in a transformation as profound as the one experienced in agriculture earlier this century when machines boosted production, displacing millions of farmers.

Many jobs are never coming back. Blue-collar workers, secretaries, receptionists, clerical workers, sales clerks, bank tellers, telephone operators, librarians, wholesalers and middle managers are just a few of the many occupations destined for virtual extinction.

Earlier industrial technologies replaced the physical power of human labour, substituting machines for body and brawn. The new computer-based technologies promise a replacement of the human mind itself, substituting thinking machines for human beings across the entire gamut of economic activity.

The implications are profound.

The restructuring of work is most apparent in the manufacturing sector. The number of factory workers in the United States declined from 33 per cent of the workforce to under 17 per cent in the past 30 years, even as American companies continued to increase production and output.

Automated technologies have been reducing the need for human labour in every manufacturing category. By the year 2020, less than 2 per cent of the global workforce will still be engaged in factory work. Over the next quarter century, we will see the virtual elimination of the blue-collar, mass assembly line worker from the production process.

In banking, insurance, and the wholesale and retail sectors, companies are deconstructing. They are eliminating layer after layer of management and infrastructure, replacing the traditional corporate pyramid and mass white-collar workforces with small, highly skilled professional work teams, using state-of-the-art software and telecommunication technologies.

Acknowledging that both the manufacturing and service sectors are quickly re-engineering their infrastructures and automating their production processes, many mainstream economists and politicians have turned to the emerging knowledge sector, pinning their hopes on new job opportunities along the information superhighway and in cyberspace.

While the 'knowledge sector' will create some new jobs, they will be too few to absorb the millions of workers displaced by new technologies. That's because the knowledge sector is, by nature, an elite workforce and not a mass labour workforce.

In the past, when new technologies dramatically increased productivity—for example in the 1920s when oil, electricity, and the assembly line replaced coal and steam-powered plants—workers sought a share of the productivity gains and organised collectively to demand a shorter working week and better pay and benefits.

It is, perhaps, predictable that not a single leading advocate of Information Age technologies has even hinted at the possibility that we might benefit from the array of new labour-saving technologies with a radically reduced working week. Instead of shortening the working week, employers are shortening the workforce—effectively preventing millions of workers from enjoying any of the benefits of the new technology revolution.

We are overdue for a debate in every country on shortening the working week to 30 hours by the year 2005, to accommodate the new reality of the Information Age economy. New labour-saving technologies, after all, are supposed to free us for greater leisure, not less pay and growing underemployment and unemployment.

Of course, employers will argue that shortening the working week and sharing the productivity gains with their workers will be too costly and threaten their ability to ▶

compete both domestically and abroad.

That need not be so. Companies like Hewlett Packard in France and BMW in Germany have reduced their working week from 37 to 31 hours while continuing to pay workers at the 37–hour rate. In return, the workers have agreed to work shifts. Management reasoned that if it could keep the new high-tech plants operating on a 24–hour basis they could double or triple productivity and thus afford to pay workers more for working less time.

In France, Government officials are playing with the idea of offering to pay the payroll taxes for the employer if management voluntarily reduces the working week. While the Government will lose tax revenue upfront, economists argue that it will make up the difference on the backside. At a reduced working week, more people will be working. Fewer people will be on welfare. And the new workers will have purchasing power and be taxpayers, all of which will benefit employers, the French economy, and the Government.

In Australia, thought might also be given to extending tax credits for any company willing to do three things: voluntarily reduce its working week; implement a profit-sharing plan so that its employees will benefit directly in the productivity gains brought on by the Information Age; and agree to a formula by which compensation to top management and shareholder dividends are not disproportionate to the benefits distributed to the rest of the company's workforce.

The 30–hour working week ought to become a rallying cry for millions of Australian workers.

Shorter working weeks, more leisure, and better pay and benefits were the benchmarks for measuring the success of the Industrial Age in the past century. We should demand no less of the Information Age in the coming century.

But even with a much reduced working week, Australia and every nation is going to have to address the problem of finding alternative forms of work for the millions of people who are no longer needed to produce the goods and services of an increasingly automated market economy.

Up to now, the marketplace and Government have been looked to, almost exclusively, for solutions to the growing economic crisis facing the country. Today, with the formal economy less able to provide permanent jobs for the millions of Australians in search of employment and with the Government retreating from its traditional role of employer of last resort, the nation's non-profit sector—the Civil Society—may be the best hope for absorbing the millions of displaced workers cast off by corporate and government re-engineering

Re-envisioning work, however, requires that we rethink our notion of politics. While politicians traditionally divide Australia into a polar spectrum running from the marketplace, on one side, to the Government, on the other, it is more accurate to think of society as a three-legged stool made up of the market sector, government sector and civil sector.

Up to now, however, the millions of people who either volunteer or work in the civil sector have not seen themselves as part of a potentially powerful constituency—one

that, if politicised, could help reshape the national agenda. Participants in the Civil Society come from every race and ethnic background, and from every class and walk of life. The one thing they share is a belief in the importance of service to the community and the creation of social capital.

If that powerful shared value can be transformed into a sense of common purpose and identity, we could redraw the political map.

Mobilising these millions of people into a broad-based social movement that can make tough demands on both the market and public sectors will be the critical test of the new politics of social capital.

The ever-deepening problem of rising productivity in the face of declining wages and vanishing jobs is likely to be one of the defining issues in every country in the years ahead.

The growing social unrest and increasing political destabilisation arising from this historic shift in the way the world does work is forcing activists of every stripe and persuasion, as well as politicians and political parties, to search for a 'radical new centre' that speaks to the concerns and aspirations of a majority of the electorate.

Redirecting the political debate to a tripartite model, with the Civil Society in the centre between the market and government spheres, fundamentally changes the nature of political discourse, opening up the possibility of re-envisioning politics, the economy and the nature of work and society in new ways in the coming century.

Sydney Morning Herald
19 June 1996

anthropologists, meals do not simply fulfil biological requirements, but are important symbolic experiences or *rituals*, where identities are created and affirmed. Family meals are an example of such rituals. What sorts of identities are affirmed through family meals? Are these, and other forms of ritual, becoming less and less a part of family experience?

5. In the 1960s and 1970s the image of the family in popular culture was captured by the TV series 'The Brady Bunch'. Here father knew best, mother was all-wise, and by the end of the show the children had learnt a lesson. There was almost total correspondence between the individual and their *social role*. In the 1990s the Brady family has been replaced by 'The Simpsons'. How can we interpret this shift sociologically?

The uncertain family

By KEVIN McDONALD

Thirty years ago the family was held up as a symbol of the social order. The family seemed to be structured in terms of norms and roles, it was organised in terms of a hierarchy. This family was a symbol of social order, reproduced at each meal with father at the head of the table, or when children were told that they were to be seen and not heard (just as workers were told that they are paid to work, not to think). It was only with the last census that we were no longer required to nominate the 'head of the household'.

As an institution, the family was seen as existing to regulate childbirth and sexuality and to socialise children into the norms and forms of authority that would allow them to be useful members of society. The culture of this family was fundamentally one of obedience. We can see these themes as central to the model of family which became consolidated in the postwar period. At the beginning of the 1950s only 4% of births took place outside marriage, and almost all people of marriageable age in fact married. Social pressures or norms were strong—estimates suggest that about 25% of couples who married in Australia in the 1950s were pregnant at the time of their marriage (suggesting that while it may have

succeeded in regulating childbirth, the institutional family was less than successful in regulating sexuality . . .).

The State was actively involved in consolidating this family, part of strategies of nation building, of 'populate or perish'. While quite new in many ways (the marriage boom having only really begun in the 1930s), the nuclear family that was consolidated in the 1950s represented a social institution organised in terms of norms and roles.

Not surprisingly, this family was a target for the social and cultural movements of the 1960s and 1970s. From the viewpoint of the 1990s, the change in patterns is truly remarkable. If during the 1950s the reality of sex before marriage was denied through hastily arranged marriages, in the 1990s some 60% of couples live together before marriage. From seriously deviant, cohabitation is now the majority experience. If 4% of births took place outside marriage in the 1950s, now 25% of births are what was once called 'illegitimate'. This means that something in the order of 40% of first births now take place outside marriage.

This really does point to a sociocultural mutation. How can we make sense of it? Researchers at the Australian Institute of Family Stud-

ies argue that these demographic shifts point to the emergence of a culture of autonomy, where the search for individual freedom has replaced an older model of doing what was expected. There can be little doubt that this is happening; that we are witnessing the emergence of a form of individuality seeking fulfilment through human relationships rather than experience constructed in terms of fulfilling social roles and expectations. This same individualism is central to cultural mutations occurring within families, such as the decline of the model of authoritarian father, the meanings of paid employment for women, and the emphasis on private space within the family, a development which has accompanied the pattern of children increasingly having their own room rather than sharing (a result of larger houses and smaller family size). But this only seems to be half the story.

The paradox

This search for autonomy and fulfilment through personal relationship is at the centre of the deinstitutionalisation of the family, defining a new context where people increasingly interact as individuals rather than as social roles. It seems to make sense, and appears to be a form of liberation when ▶

contrasted with the constraints of the earlier model of family as institution.

But while the demographers suggest a shift to family patterns organised in terms of individual autonomy, we are continually confronted with images and stories of an 'epidemic' of child abuse. Images of predatory paedophiles dominate the national press and television. Child abuse appears as rampant. Claims are made that child sexual abuse, a code for the return of the question of incest, is widespread. One recent feature on 'our betrayed children' in the *Age* tells us that while 2% of biological fathers engage in incest, 10% of de facto or stepfathers enter into incestuous relationships.

This is not purely a fabrication of the current generation of moral campaigners. In Australia notifications of child abuse increased tenfold over the period 1980–1990, and we have witnessed the emergence of the new category of children 'at risk'—meaning fundamentally at risk in the family.

But alongside of this image of the dysfunctional family, we are also witnessing the emergence of a new middle-class model as well. Here interaction in terms of roles and obedience is giving way to relationships of dialogue and negotiation. The term 'obedience', once a way of grasping the relationship between adults and children, now only applies to the family dog.

The institutional family seems to be bifurcating, giving way to the dysfunctional family on the one hand, and to the new negotiating family on the other.

Welfare theorists like Adam Jamrozik argue that the uncertainty around the family is fundamentally to be understood in terms of the question of social class. As he

points out, the massive majority of child abuse cases reported to the State and acted upon are among the poor, and he argues that the State impact on the family is bifurcating along class lines—with family services to the working class increasingly focused almost entirely on 'child protection', while services to the middle class take the form of subsidised 'child care'. As Jamrozik argues, in this bifurcated model, child care has increasingly become claimable only by families where both parents are in the labour market, while the rates of employment of women in the poorest half of the population have actually declined over the past two decades. The abuse epidemic approach increases this pathologisation, locating socio-cultural problems in the dysfunctional family, rather than envisaging modes of social support for parents and children beyond the current approach defined uniquely in terms of labour market policy.

But arguably there is something more complex occurring as well. The class analysis underlines important themes, but it is weak in terms of socio-cultural transformation. If the authoritarian family appears to be giving way to the disorganised and increasingly dysfunctional family, there is increasing uncertainty around the emergent middle class model as well. La Trobe University sociologist Beryl Langer underlines the degree of anxiety amongst middle-class parents who increasingly understand the world in terms of the imperatives of success and so increasingly look upon child rearing as an exercise in mobilising the potential of the child. Tradition is rejected as unable to cope with the world of uncertainty, so increasing recourse is made to parenting manuals and to educational games

that will give the toddler a head start in the race of life. As Langer argues, these parents see the future of their child in terms of success or alienation, and are motivated more by fear that their child may become a loser rather than by the exercise of parental roles.

Problems of personhood

The family experience remains fundamentally one of 'individuation', one where the person becomes a human subject. We can see this beginning from the period when the child first says no! to its parents, with subjectivity constructed both in terms of identification and distance.

At a cultural level the disorganisation of the institutional family and of the rites of passage associated with it means that at crucial points this experience is becoming unclear. We can see this in the increasing concern with the self-esteem of children, and the increasing recourse to American feel-good programmes aimed at boosting children's self-esteem in schools. Similar questions are at stake in emerging cultural uncertainties around adolescence—evident from the increasing incidence of forms of addictive experience such as eating disorders, to the search for forms of risk in a culture without rites of passage that leads to the high incidence of injury and death among young men driving cars.

These are complex issues, but there is a sense that they converge in the contemporary family experience. The relationship between children and adults is doubly uncertain. While the cultural importance of contemporary individualism undermines older models of parental authority, the cultural meanings of childhood are increasingly unclear. On the one hand children ▶

enter the adult cultural world at an earlier age, so that the period of childhood is being culturally shortened—this is evident in sex education and sexual practice. But the entry into the adult social world, defined through employment and establishing an independent household, is increasingly delayed. Something of this cultural uncertainty is evident when one can purchase condoms at the age of twelve or thirteen, but not cigarettes until the age of eighteen. The idea of maturing as entry into a coherent adult world makes no sense in this context.

The abuse epidemic, which has reached a peak with apocalyptic images of predators and paedophiles, beyond the pathologisation and bifurcation that it represents, points above all to a culture increasingly confronted with questions of personhood on the one hand, and to a context where the experience of vulnerability is understood in terms of victimhood on the other. There is a cultural parallel between the images of crack cocaine and the paedophile. Both point to real problems, but neither is the cause.

Arena Magazine
Issue 23, June–July 1996

Questions

1. Sociology has approached the family as an institution, a form of social experience that socialises through transmitting norms, where individuals become social selves through learning social roles. The institutional family regulates identities and experience, and is structured in terms of gender and generation roles. This article suggests that new themes in family experience are emerging, which represent a *deinstitutionalisation* of the family, whereby interaction in families is increasingly less structured in terms of roles and statuses (positions). What is the evidence provided for this, and how convincing is it?

2. To what extent does your family experience correspond to this model of the deinstitutionalising family?

3. This article suggests that we are witnessing a shift from the institutional family, organised in terms of roles and statuses, to an emphasis on individuals and the relationships between them. It is suggested that this has lead to the emergence of two new family forms—the negotiating family, and the destructured dysfunctional family. What evidence is put forward for this, and how strong is it?

4. Are *middle-class* parents increasingly concerned with the success of their children to the point where older models of parenting based on social roles and norms are being replaced by 'strategic parenting' and the fear that their child may become a loser in an ever more intensely competitive society?

5. How extensive is the evidence supporting the claim that we are experiencing widespread cultural concern with *self-esteem*?

6. To what extent can this concern about self-esteem be understood in terms of the decline of social roles as a means of structuring self-identity, and as the darker side of the culture of autonomy and self-creation?

7. Are we witnessing a *moral panic* regarding the place of children in contemporary society? If this panic does exist, what are the most convincing sociological explanations for it?

OVER TO YOU

Identify one of the sociological hypotheses in these two articles, such as the deinstitutionalisation of the family. Identify what this might involve, and then test this through interviewing parents or older children about their family experiences. Present your results to your tutorial group.

Youth and the family

Teenagers seek sanctuary in tribes from the ghetto

By MEGAN JONES

Australian teenagers have a tendency towards racism and wish their parents would grow up and stop acting like children, a global survey suggests. The Teenmood Study, by one of the world's largest advertising agencies, True North Communications, investigated the attitudes and behaviour of teenagers in 20 countries.

The study describes Australian teenagers as belonging to the 'ACES' generation: alienated, cynical, experimental and savvy.

Teenagers converse globally on the Internet, but find sanctuary in their bedrooms and in the customs, dress and folklore of their tribes—homies, surfies, grungists and yuppie wanna-bes.

The survey found teenagers are pessimistic and do not trust anyone in authority. They do not want their parents to be their friends and they want them to grow old gracefully.

A managing partner of True North's Mojo Partners Australia, Mr Nicholas Davie, said the survey found teenagers lacked rites of passage into adulthood.

'They have no benchmarks of their own progress because the generations which went before them are stubbornly holding on to their own—blue jeans, rock'n'roll and smoking marijuana.' The survey found traditional institutions had let down teenagers.

'The home used to be their haven. But with the breakdown of the nuclear family, it has shrunk to their bedroom, which has become their sanctuary, their biosphere,' Mr Davie said.

'Parents are holding on to the traditional teenage values and behaviour such as wearing jeans, doing drugs, listening to rock music, binge drinking and body piercing, all of which were associated with the rebellious teenagers.'

With adults trying to stay forever young, teenagers have been forced to substitute tribal values for family values.

'The kids are frustrated because they want to be rebellious but have no common enemy and no unifying causes.' Since adults have deprived the next generation of a dominant youth culture, teenagers have divided into tribes whose values and behaviour come from the Hispanic and black ghettos of America.

The survey noted Australian teenagers have a tendency towards racism, but not based on colour, as in other countries. 'It's based on immigration, but it has nothing to do with colour,' Mr Davie said. 'It is to do with educational opportunities.' Thanks to the Asian study ethic, more Asian students were taking places at universities and teenagers resented Asians having the opportunities. On the domestic front the survey found teenagers more intelligent, worldly and streetwise than their parents at the same age.

Mr Davie said teenagers were initiated into many attitudes by 'street kids'—who the study describes as 'waifs madly trying to give themselves definition'.

Australian teenagers are . . .
- Alienated.
- Cynical.
- Experimental.
- Savvy.
- Pessimistic.
- Brutally honest.
- Self-reliant.
- Technologically smart.
- Lowering expectations of their own success.
- Global thinkers.

Source: The Teenmood Study.

The Age
8 August 1996

Questions

1. What are the major transformations of the family that Megan Jones points to?

2. The Durkheimian tradition in sociology argues that identities are constructed through *symbolic boundaries*, through creating oppositions between 'them' and 'us'. What are examples of such symbolic boundaries?

3. This article points to a decline in generational identities, and a difficulty for young people to construct a sense of 'us' opposed to an older generation. Why does Jones argue this?

4. What are *rites of passage*? Do young people need these to make sense of their experiences?

OVER TO YOU

Interview a group of teenagers about their experience of the shift from childhood to adulthood. (They will need to be over 15, or you will need to ensure that you get parental approval.) Explore the ways in which they construct an 'us' identity, and give particular attention to whether they speak of 'them'— other social groups that may point to symbolic boundaries. Are we witnessing the end of generation conflict, and the ways of constructing identity associated with it?

Reproduction—social or biological?

The marriage market

By BETTINA ARNDT

Marriage is changing in Australia today. AGB McNair conducted research to monitor changing attitudes and analysed the statistics to show just how patterns are shifting. Hundreds of people were surveyed—from the elite through to the struggling.

What emerges is a remarkable picture of marriage in flux. Significant changes are occurring in the way people choose marriage partners. More women are marrying younger men and, particularly in the lower socio-economic groups, there are more women marrying down.

But at the top end, women are behaving very differently. Many elite women cling to the traditional marriage gradient, seeking only high-status men. In doing so, they condemn themselves to having their careers derailed as a result of child-rearing and home responsibilities. The fascinating reasons for their choices have bearing on some of the most critical issues in marriage today.

'I want someone to come up to my level. Why would I take anything less? A professional person? Definitely. And intelligent. Preferably with a good tertiary background. Money? If not the same, then more. I couldn't respect anyone who earned less than me,' [says] Jan Seveirie, a tertiary-educated immigration officer.

'I'm an education snob. I couldn't imagine being married to anyone whom I couldn't talk to about my work. He would have to be educated in some way, if not similarly qualified,' [says] Nicola Palmer, a Sydney investment banker.

Here are the women who are driving some of the most dramatic changes in the marriage market. These well-educated, successful women know what they want. Most are seeking men just like themselves.

It wasn't so long ago that successful educated men spread themselves around. Thirty years ago, men with degrees only occasionally married similarly well-educated women. When we look at couples married before 1950, surveyed in the Australian Bureau of Statistics (ABS) 1992 Family Survey, only 10 per cent of the couples in which the males had degrees had equally well-educated wives. Most men married down.

Social class was, of course, a critical issue. Successful men were more likely to marry women from the right families, the daughters of prominent men. To be born into the right family was once qualification enough to be considered a desirable bride.

But it is changing. Women are now able to achieve social status through their own achievements and then marry across—choosing equally successful men.

Increasingly, men and women meet their partners in the course of their education or through the workplace, where intimacy develops naturally through shared experience. In fact, in many high-pressure jobs, there may be little opportunity for conducting a social life elsewhere.

The 1992 Family Survey showed that, in the most recent batch of marriages, couples marrying in 1980 or later, there were 103,400

couples (7 per cent) where both partners had a university degree or higher and 200,000 couples (15 per cent) where only one partner had a degree. But almost half (46 per cent) of the male graduates were married to female graduates.

When the university-educated, successful women were asked about the type they would consider marrying, most expressed a preference for professional men with good incomes and tertiary education. Naturally other factors were important as well—personality, humour, sensitivity and faithfulness, a hot issue for some women. But most were clearly intent on marrying across, if not up.

There were some exceptions. 'I wouldn't care if he was a labourer. Personality and overall attractiveness, physical and mental, are what matter most,' said Helen*, a 31-year-old Melbourne accountant. But she wasn't sure it would prove to be a good match. 'I think a lot of men feel inferior if a woman is more intelligent or earning more. They are more likely to be attracted to someone below them. They like to be on a pedestal.'

Shelley Lipe, a 34-year-old Melbourne lawyer, knows what it is like to go out with a less successful man. 'Guys without a good job have an inferiority complex. It causes real problems because they don't want to associate with your friends or mix with your family. They don't feel right. You feel the social pressures. "Who's Shelley going out with?" "Oh, is that what he does. Not as good as her last one."'

The reaction of friends proved a very strong theme, particularly in ▶

the women's groups. Many women were clearly nervous of their peers' reaction to a boyfriend who didn't fit in, a man they judged as not good enough. It was intriguing to discover the quest for friends' approval as one of the forces driving women's push for high-status men.

What about the men? Well, the professional, high-income men were very aware they had to pass certain hurdles to get to first base with many women. Men who lack the attributes sought by successful women were very aware that they didn't come up to scratch. 'I find the career woman is looking for something above myself. I don't come up to her standard,' said Frank Preusche, 40, a divorced Melbourne man working in the Department of Defence.

Overall, there was a striking lack of consensus among the men. Some clearly still prefer to marry down, while other professional men see it as natural that they should choose women more like themselves. 'I think it's much more likely now men would marry their peers, not only peers in a professional sense but in an intellectual sense,' said Bob*, 38, a high-ranking Canberra public servant.

The question of who cares for the children in a dual-career family is clearly troubling some men, but it may be becoming less acceptable to express such concerns—or so it appeared when I talked to David*, a 26–year-old Sydney investment banker. David mentioned a conversation he had recently with some friends.

'I told them I could see myself in five or six years' time marrying a teacher or perhaps a nurse. Someone who, in my mind, would be a great partner, would have her own profession but would also be willing to look after the kids.'

His friends' reaction? 'They laughed. They viewed it as though it was aiming a bit too low. As though it was easy prey rather than challenging myself.' David got the message that ambitious professional men are now expected to seek high-status women. But he's still attracted to the idea of a less career-oriented woman: 'I think it would make for a happy home life.'
* Some people interviewed preferred to remain anonymous.

Sydney Morning Herald
22 June 1996

Questions

1. Are marriages between people in upper socio-economic groups becoming more 'open' or more 'closed'? What does the ABS data indicate?

2. What might explain why marriage patterns are changing among women in lower socio-economic groups?

3. Sociologists use the term 'homogamy' to describe the process whereby people tend to choose a partner from their own social group. This involves the social actors interpreting social characteristics as personality characteristics which they find attractive in a partner. For example, when Nicola, an investment banker, says 'I couldn't imagine being married to anyone whom I couldn't talk to about my work. He would have to be educated', is this a characteristic of personality, or of membership in a social group?

4. Shelley, a lawyer, talks of the difficulties in going out with a less successful man, saying: 'You feel the social pressures. "Oh, is that what he does. Not as good as her last one."' These social pressures are an example of what sociologists call group *closure*. What are other examples of such closure in this article? How pervasive are such forms of group closure in your experience?

5. What are the main changes occurring in gender relationships that we can identify through this experience?

Can we alter our basic urges?

By PAUL DAVIES

Why do pretty young women marry rich old men? Cynics dismiss such matches as calculated manipulation: the rich man regards the woman as a trophy symbolising his wealth and status, while the woman secures a comfortable lifestyle and the chance of a big inheritance. ▶

However, such pat explanations are being increasingly challenged by biologists who claim that much of our sexual behaviour is essentially programmed by Darwinian evolution, and that many social institutions and practices such as marriage, courtship and family structure owe a lot to ancient biological urge.

Genes do more than determine our physical appearance; they also play a role in behaviour. And genes are in the business of replicating. Those genes that are poor replicators soon disappear, as they are less likely to make it to the next generation. Consequently, much of what we do, despite any beliefs we may harbour about free will, is actually a slavish response to our genes trying to reproduce themselves.

When our genes talk to us, we often react subconsciously. Men are attracted to women with big breasts, wide hips and narrow waists without needing to rationalise the child rearing implications of this anatomy. The same men may act aggressively or show off in fancy cars on an instinctive attempt to impress women with their status.

Such basic urges are ingrained in human nature. Decades of feminist thought and social philosophy have made little difference. Take any society on earth and find a rich or powerful man in his 50s—film star, politician, businessman—and the chances are high that he will be in the company of an attractive woman decades younger. Indeed, we need look no further than our own universities to witness the familiar phenomenon of the male professor replacing his ageing wife with a young student.

Biologists are not surprised by this. A young woman's genes are most likely to survive if her babies are well looked after, so it makes sense for her to find a partner with good resources. This normally means a high-status male with power and wealth. Obviously he is likely to be much older than her. Again the genetic urges may express themselves unconsciously. Research suggests that women do not seek out such matches as a deliberate strategy; their genes ensure that they will find power and wealth an aphrodisiac.

Because women invest so much time and physical effort in child-rearing, it is understandable that their choice of partner is dictated primarily by the need for a well resourced and stable home. For a man, however, the optimum strategy is quite opposite. Gene-wise, it pays for him to impregnate as many women as possible. After all, sperm is cheap and plentiful . . .

So are we all doomed to act out a pre-programmed genetic agenda that all too often serves to make men and women miserable or can human beings successfully override their genetic legacy? Alas, the statistical evidence suggests that whatever the prevailing social or religious norms, our genes manage to manipulate us with surprising efficiency. We may not be able to alter human sexual behaviour much, but at least it helps to understand how it originated.

Paul Davies is a physicist and author.

The Australian
14 August 1996

Questions

1. If sexual desire were shaped by genes, we would expect a similarity of desired physical forms across time and across different societies and cultures. Are forms of the erotic and sexual desire essentially the same across societies, in the way that a genetic determinist argument would suggest?

2. Are 'big breasts, wide hips and narrow waists' important anatomically for child rearing?

3. Paul Davies suggests that a woman's choice of partner is dictated primarily by the need for a well-resourced and stable home, while for a man a genetic strategy will lead him to seek to impregnate as many women as possible. This suggests that men have a greater proclivity to sexual activity, and this is driven genetically. Has this view of the sexes been constant across Western history? Does it characterise all societies, or is Davies interpreting social and cultural patterns as genetic universals?

OVER TO YOU

Explore the relationship between processes of group closure and gender. Interview people about the characteristics and qualities they are looking for in a partner. To what extent are these social characteristics interpreted as individual or psychological traits? What sorts of social class and gender relationships do they point to? Present your results to your tutorial group.

12 Gender and work

Women do twice the housework, and don't mind

By ALICIA LARRIERA

Women are spending more than twice as much time as their partners each week keeping the house and children in running order—yet almost half are untroubled by this 'clearly inequitable' division of housework, a study has found.

Not surprisingly, men report high levels of satisfaction with the fact they spend a mean of 16.8 hours a week devoted to housework, compared with the 42.7 hours a week clocked up by their partners.

However, the researchers, Janeen Baxter and Mark Western, of the Research School of Social Science at the Australian National University, whose findings were presented yesterday to the Fifth Australian Family Research Conference in Brisbane, were surprised to discover that almost half of the women seemed untroubled by their lot.

Their explanation for the apparent paradox was that most men and women still believe that housework and child care are women's responsibility.

They say this makes it difficult to envisage alternatives to arrangements that are seen as 'natural and inevitable'.

'Furthermore, there is little evidence that these patterns have changed over the last seven years and little reason to expect that they will change greatly over the next few years.

'The explanation seems to lie in gender role attitudes and the extent to which men participate in non-traditional tasks.

'Moreover, if men participate in some conventional female chores, women are likely to feel that their partners are contributing above and beyond normal expectations and hence are likely to feel more satisfied than those women whose partners do not contribute in non-conventional areas.'

According to the research, if men help out in cleaning-up after meals, doing some ironing or taking in the washing, this is sufficient to increase women's satisfaction with their lot—even if they still do twice as much work.

The research paper, *Satisfaction with Housework: Explaining the Paradox*, reports that a clear divi-

sion of labour along traditional lines—with men participating in most outdoor work and women taking primary responsibility for child care and indoor activities such as cooking, cleaning and laundry—has remained unchanged for the past seven years.

But the researchers say their findings do not imply that women enjoy doing housework—they may recognise the division of labour is unfair, and not enjoy it, but may still be satisfied with the current arrangements.

Sydney Morning Herald
30 November 1996

HOUSEWORK WHO DOES IT (Hours per week)

	WOMEN	MEN
Preparing meals	11.9	3.1
Cleaning up after meals	6.8	2.7
Grocery shopping	3.1	1.5
Cleaning house	9.2	1.8
Taking out garbage	0.4	0.5
Washing	5.1	0.8
Home maintenance/Improvement	0.9	3.0
Mowing lawns	0.5	1.3
Gardening	2.4	2.5
Ironing	3.0	0.3
TOTAL HOURS	42.7	16.8

Source: ANU.

Sex roles still rule work

By JOANNE PAINTER

The distinction between men's and women's work is alive and well, particularly in blue-collar occupations, according to a new study.

A national study of work and identity has found that in some instances, men deliberately preserved male-only occupations to buttress their notions of masculinity and femininity.

This was particularly true in the trades, where many men drew a direct link between their gender-dominated skill and their personal masculinity.

The work ethic is also thriving ▶

in Australia. According to the final draft of *The Work Generation*, by Professor Belinda Probert and Fiona Macdonald from RMIT, Australians demonstrate a 'remarkable degree of commitment to paid work'.

Although motivated by different experiences and needs, the sense of identity of many Australians was inextricably tied up with their paid and unpaid work.

The study was part of the Brotherhood of St Laurence's Future of Work project, examining the changes reshaping work in Australia and their implications.

For groups such as nurses, teachers and child-care workers, the loss of paid work was a major threat to life satisfaction.

And while the influx of women into the workforce has eroded many distinctions between male and female jobs over the past 20 years, big differences remain in the way men and women achieve satisfaction from their jobs.

For example, many men gained satisfaction from working outside or working with their hands. By contrast, many of the women surveyed linked satisfaction to learning new skills or the social interaction of the workplace. Other women valued not having to take work home with them and the opportunity to focus on activities outside work.

And for many women, 'family work' continues to be an important source of identity and satisfaction. 'For these women, their satisfaction derived directly from the love they received from their children. A smile from a young child was enough to compensate for a hard day,' the report said.

But this view was not held by many older mothers, who spoke of being 'mum's taxi' and a 'slave'.

Not surprisingly, many older workers and those in regional centres with high unemployment valued security and stability highly.

What workers hated most included highly repetitive tasks, working under close supervision and the lack of career development.

Working hours was also a big issue for Australian men and women.

According to the report's authors, overwork was mentioned in almost every interview with full-time workers.

Work and identity

- Many people regard having a job as an individual's moral obligation.
- Paid and unpaid employment is the major mechanism for integrating people into society.
- Most men see paid employment as confirmation of their role as providers.
- Many women define themselves in terms of being a mother; most men surveyed described themselves primarily in terms of their role as provider.

Source: The Work Generation.

The Age
7 October 1996

Questions

1. Even where men and women in households are both in full-time employment, women undertake approximately three times more housework than men. Is this an example of *patriarchy*?

2. Examine the detailed breakdown of housework distribution. What makes a task a male or female one?

3. Sociologists like Erving Goffman argue that social life is *performance*, and that the social actor with power in a situation will most likely be the one that is symbolically central. Is audience and performance relevant to the way housework is divided? Consider the situation where men and women share the cooking as an example.

4. Traditional gender roles are more prevalent among those groups who are less successful in the market—among working-class blue-collar workers, and in working-class families. Might this reflect their distance from the new models of competitive masculinity and femininity associated with cultural and economic elites? How might the distribution of social class patterns influence gender patterns in terms of work?

5. What are the main areas in which women are involved in paid employment in Australia? To what extent do these patterns reflect the transfer of traditional gender roles into the workplace?

OVER TO YOU

How can we explore the meanings of household work? Interview both genders about their experience of housework, if possible from different socio-economic groups. What patterns emerge? Offer an interpretation to your tutorial group.

13 Gender redefinitions

A nip, tuck or jab to roll away the years

By NARELLE HOOPER

Twice a year, advertising agency chief Ralph Jones slips away from his office to have a collagen top-up, a treatment that helps hold his wrinkles at bay. Half an hour later, with just a few red needle marks showing, he is back at work, about one millilitre of bovine collagen plumping up the lines around his eyes, mouth, cheeks and chin.

The procedure, which costs about $500, takes years off his appearance. Jones, 43, who, like other executives interviewed for this story, does not want his real name revealed, frankly admits that vanity prompted him to opt for collagen.

'I thought I was starting to look my age,' he says.

Ageing can be depressing, especially when you hear Sydney cosmetic surgeon Dr Geoffrey Heber describe the changes wrought by time and the elements: droopy eyelids, sagging jowls, red-veined noses and cheeks, crow's feet, sleep lines, eye bags and thinning, yellowing, blotchy skin. That's even before you hit that sensitive hairline—as a rule of thumb, by age 50 about half all males will have lost much of their hair.

And specialists like Heber are exercising their smile lines all the way to the bank as more men put aside their reservations and line up for the discreet nip, tuck or jab that offer hope of recapturing lost youth. In the past five years, with a bumper crop of baby boomers creeping towards the half-century and in an era when fashion and image rule, the business that panders to male vanity has taken off.

Heber says cosmetic procedures are more widely acceptable today. In some areas of his practice, more than 20% of clients are men. Melbourne plastic surgeon Leo Rozner says that in five years men have grown from 2% of his clients to around 25%. Cosmetic treatment, Heber says, is 'not seen as manly. It's showing vulnerability.' But, he adds: 'That attitude is changing.'

The pressures of today's corporate environment on executives to perform better than their predecessors, he says, has prompted many to seek treatment. However, they tend not to talk about it. Heber says there are also workforce pressures 'where you may be chucked on the scrap heap at 50' and 'people think if you are older you look less dynamic'.

At the Sydney clinic that Heber and wife Deborah Davis run from their home in Annandale clients have to wait 10 weeks simply to make a booking. The real problem, Heber says, is coping with demand.

Some of the finer details of what is involved hardly bear thinking about. The creamy collagen that is injected comes from the hides of dead cows.

Nurse and collagen-injection specialist Susan Ellis, says 'appearance is important'. She had her first collagen injection 13 years ago while working for a plastic surgeon. She says it costs about $240, with most people needing a top-up every four or five months.

Ellis, who trains doctors in injection procedures, says the number of heterosexual men seeking the treatment, mainly for frown or smile lines, is growing.

A large proportion of her clientele are female executives in their late 30s and 40s. A national sales manager with a cosmetics company went one step further. The executive, 50, had the edges of her lips plumped out. The procedure involves a fine length of teflon fibre being threaded through a needle and sewn into the outline around the lips from corner to corner. It cost the executive $1200.

After two years pulling faces in front of the mirror, Ed Brown had to agree with his young wife: he did look tired—and saggy. Nearly 12 months and $20,000 worth of cosmetic surgery later, the chemical-import company owner, 59, looks like a new man. 'People used to say, "Gee, you look tired", but I felt good,' says Brown (not his real name).

Brown chose a partial facelift. After three hours under the scalpel of a Melbourne plastic surgeon and a few weeks out of the public eye, he looked about 10 years younger.

Now he will admit that, for someone who, when he was young, blanched at the thought of even using a male deodorant, his resort to cosmetic surgery was a dramatic step. 'I had a lot of reservations,' he says.

Brown, so preoccupied by what lay ahead, says he had a rush of mild panic when, just after his premed, his mobile phone rang—he was being pressed to make a decision on a deal. Next day, 'with a head like a balloon', he was back in contact with his office on his mobile. Within a week the swelling was gone and only the bruising and stitches were evident. The stitches came out after 10 days and Brown was back in his office ▶

within a couple of weeks, a newly cultivated five o'clock shadow covering remaining marks.

Brown, delighted with the results, says: 'The change was remarkable.

It's an absolute uplift of the spirit and face.' The main change he says is that he feels more confident with his younger management team because in his position,

'you tend to get treated as an old man'.

Business Review Weekly
18 November 1996

Questions

1. The rise of cosmetic surgery amongst men has been cited as an indicator of *androgyny*—a blurring of the boundaries of masculine and feminine in contemporary culture. This article casts some light on new forms of masculinity: what social groups are most likely to be seeking cosmetic surgery, and for what reasons?

2. Many of the men interviewed here link the way they look to increasing imperatives of competition in the workplace. Do these developments point to an extension of models of 'vanity', or to a more complex set of transformations?

3. Sociological research suggests that the men who are innovating new forms of masculinity (SNAGS) are generally men who do not depend upon physical strength for their social position or status—and are typically men involved in symbolic or communication work, such as teachers and professionals. To what extent are the 'new masculinities' associated with the new middle classes and professions, or the 'new woman' associated with professionals and business women? To what extent are economically dominant groups culturally and symbolically dominant as well?

4. Does this suggest that our culture is becoming more age-phobic, where growing old is interpreted increasingly in negative terms? If so, why is it happening?

OVER TO YOU

Explore gender innovations across social groups. Undertake exploratory interviews of men and women (from different social groups if possible) about forms of practice once associated with one gender or another—use of cosmetics, child care, involvement in contact sports or body building. To what extent are gender innovations linked to social class, and do they transcend this? Present the results to your tutorial group.

14 Sexuality

Sex in the '90s

By GRETCHEN MILLER

If there is one thing for sure about sex in the 1990s, it's no longer a matter of the missionary position, wham bam, thank you ma'am. Sex these days is more complicated, and more sophisticated, than ever before, although not without its casualties.

Even mainstream advertising has taken on board the idea that sexual identity is no longer cut and dried—Ella Bache's skin fitness advertisement in magazines and on train stations features two women embracing, and the use of men who will appeal to both the gay and the women's market has been around for some time.

It is hard to tell whether the gradual mainstreaming of bisexuality is simply a fashion or a more deep-seated acceptance, says a research fellow at Macquarie University's National Centre in HIV Social Research, Mr Michael Bartos.

For homosexual men, bisexual activity used to in part stem from the social pressure of having to appear to be heterosexual. Now it's 'a notion of being more versatile', Mr Bartos says. And for women, according to a spokesman for the sex industry association, the Eros Foundation, Mr Robbie Swan, bisexuality is taking off, as evidenced by the various industry personals magazines.

'There have been an incredible amount of 20– to 40–year-old women who want to have a first-time lesbian encounter,' he says. But these women are not looking to change their sexual orientation. 'Often the women who want this are not necessarily after lesbian

(identifying) women, they're after other heterosexual women,' he says. They are often in a marriage but want to experiment, with their male partner's consent.

Women have become more aware of their bodies and their sexual health and well-being, says the director of education services for Family Planning NSW, Ms Kendra Sundquist. Young women have also come to expect that sex will be a pleasurable and satisfying experience.

While the baby boomers were the first to talk about female sexuality in an open and validating manner, Generation-X women (aged in their 20s or late teens) now have high expectations of the sexual experience, she says.

Mainstream sexual behaviour has become broad ranging—from bondage to tantric sex and sex which does not involve penetration. 'Sex to a lot of people years ago used to be missionary position,' Ms Sundquist says. 'Now there's a lot of emphasis on pleasuring—giving a much more whole body experience.'

Cosmopolitan magazine's editor-in-chief, Ms Pat Ingram, says that after several decades of talking and thinking about and being so open about sex, there is a greater acceptance of sexual diversity. But she did not believe half the female population was rushing to get into bed with other women.

Both Ms Ingram and Ms Sundquist believe monogamy is becoming more popular, with media attention not just on sex but on dealing with relationships. 'Women are trying to understand men a little

more and men are trying to understand women . . . I think that probably tends to make relationships easier to work at as well,' she says.

Mr Swan says that while the over-55s are a sexually conservative group, it is the 30-and 40-year-olds who are most interested in experimentation. 'I suspect those people are the ones who encountered sex (for the first time) in the '60s. Whilst these people had babies and raised families in the '80s and late '70s, now the kids have grown up a bit they have regained that freedom,' he says.

'People over 55 are still having a lot of sex, but they're just not experimental.' But those around 30 and 40 years old are keen to try different things. Sex-aid advertising has taken off in the classified section of *Cosmopolitan*, Ms Ingram says. While not all the magazine's readers are interested, many do enjoy them.

'Obviously it has grown—I guess more shops blatantly promote that stuff to women.'

Mr Swan says the manufacture of sex aids has changed substantially. Sex toys were becoming very sophisticated and very woman-oriented. 'They are just designed to touch all the right spots.'

Safe sex has followed suit. Between 1985 and 1994, Ansell's condom sales have jumped from 140,000 to 300,000. 'There's no doubt that the safe sex market is becoming much more sophisticated as well—(some) women are choosing vibrators rather than having one-night stands,' Mr Swan says.

There were more than 1 million vibrators sold last year, and he ▶

estimated there are '8 million (vibrators) currently humming away there in Australia'.

According to sex researcher and spokeswoman for the Prostitutes Rights Organisation for Sex Workers, Ms Roberta Perkins, the number of men using prostitutes has dropped from 16 per cent of the population in the 1940s, to 3 per cent in the mid-1990s. She says this has partly to do with the legalisation of prostitution—the sense of doing something 'naughty' has evaporated. 'The danger and allure goes,' she says.

But sexual practice has diversified—in the 1960s and '70s a man asking for oral sex would have been beaten up by a pimp. Now light bondage is de rigueur and there are four or five brothels specialising in bondage around Sydney.

Ms Sundquist says that while the age of virginity loss has not changed over the past decade (by the age of 17 about 50 per cent of teenagers have had their first sexual intercourse) teenage sex has also become more sophisticated.

Oral sex is common: 'It's a way of having good sex but (low risk)—it's very sophisticated,' she says. Relationships tend to fall into a serial monogamy pattern and last just a few weeks or months. 'It's all very full on.'

While women have developed higher expectations, men have responded well to their partners' wishes, Ms Sundquist says. 'I think younger men are much more sensitive and want to satisfy their partner, and are well and truly up-to-date with what women like—and I think they want to be good at what they do,' she says.

The Generation-X gay man is significantly different from his older peers, says Mr Bartos. 'The difference is that the baby-boomer generation has actually grown up with gay liberation ... it's something very political. One of the inventions of the late '70s gay culture was the hyper-masculine clone—it was a kind of turning on its head the "gays must be sissies" (tag),' he says.

'For the Generation X-er, in a sense they have taken for granted that there is sexual diversity out there. They are also much more liable not to draw such rigid boundaries—basically to be much more fluid about gender identity ... They're also inclined to be more romantic in a way which is also in part an age thing—not to use condoms in sex because it spoils the love.'

Surprisingly, AIDS and homosexuality are gaining acceptance in the community. In a yearly study done on first-year psychology students, there has been a definite change in attitude, according to Mr Bartos.

'There's certainly been a gradual, appreciable softening of attitudes and more of a feeling that "yes, HIV is something that could happen to me",' he says.

'One of the other main findings is that there has actually been a change in discriminatory attitudes. There's substantially less willingness to discriminate against people with HIV,' Mr Bartos says.

He says there is no evidence of an increasing number of homosexuals, and contrary to popular belief, homosexual sex practices are quite similar to heterosexual sex. 'I certainly think there's a group of gay men who regard themselves as sexual aficionados and sexual adventurers, who will try anything ... but no more than 5 per cent,' he says.

'Kissing and touching are the most preferred sexual practice ... the range of what is done is in fact a fairly restricted range and is not all that different from the standard range of sexual practice for heterosexuals,' Mr Bartos says.

'Gay men like to think of themselves as possibly more sexually adventurous than they really are. I think the stigma that has been associated with homosexuality gives any homosexual sex the flavour of naughtiness.'

But amongst all the pleasure, there is a darker side to sex in the 1990s, Ms Sundquist says. 'There's some unreal expectations about what you can achieve ... People are thinking, "Everybody else is doing these fantastic things, what's wrong with me?"'

'I think people expect more, but with time constraints ... it's something you do before going to sleep or getting up—it's not exactly going on for hours,' she says.

'There's a bit of an assumption too that somehow everybody knows everything (about sex), but of course that's a huge assumption. There's a large percentage of the population that don't have access to this knowledge.'

Older people are also feeling under pressure. More older women, often those going through menopause, were seeing Family Planning about sexual difficulties. Often in older couples, confusion sets in when the male partner has suffered a retrenchment, and then might drink or smoke too much and find it difficult to get an erection. 'Women often blame themselves that they're not attractive any more,' she says.

And despite the constant presence of sex and the female body in the media, young women, sadly, still have negative feelings about menstruation.

'Even in today's liberated society there's still these myths and taboos,' Ms Sundquist says.

Sydney Morning Herald
1 August 1996

Questions

1. Sociological explorations of sexual practice underline a series of cultural shifts around the meaning of sexuality, from the decline of fear to the search for pleasure and intensity. The 'sexual revolution' of the 1960s regarded sexual activity as breaking forms of social control and challenged social *norms* and *moralisation*. This was radicalised by the gay movement of the 1970s. How can we interpret the context of the 1990s?

    Writers and social critics like Germaine Greer argue that Western culture is increasingly based on a 'masturbatory paradigm'—a culture of excitement without meaning, the search for instant pleasure from sex to phallic chocolate bars—indiscriminate and empty pleasure which sexualises food just as much as reducing eating to immediate satisfaction of appetite.

    Sociologists tend to underline the complexity and ambiguity of contemporary change. Antony Giddens in Britain argues that sexuality is at the centre of a search for authenticity and a cultural concern with intimacy. In France, Alain Touraine argues on the one hand that increasingly commodified sex (the development of the sex industry) is linked to the cult of pleasure spread by TV and video, but on the other hand, that the place of sexuality in contemporary culture also represents the search for forms of love and happiness which involve an encounter with the other.

    Max Weber believed that modern culture would become more and more instrumental and desensualised. We are witnessing a sexualisation of contemporary culture, with a break with forms of sexuality governed by fear, duty and the institutionalisation of reproduction. If the erotic means communication, does sex-as-a-commodity exemplified by 0055 numbers vindicate Weber's fear that Western culture would become focused on sensation, but desensualised?

2. How can we interpret the change in contemporary culture, where sexual identity is increasingly understood as something to be explored?

3. Western culture was shaped by strong oppositions between masculine and feminine, heterosexual and homosexual. These very strong symbolic oppositions are weakening, evident in the cultural importance of drag and the significance attached to authenticity and being true to oneself. How important are these shifts?

4. In the economy we are witnessing a decline in social regulation and the affirmation of the market as the paradigm of interaction. In the area of sexuality we are also witnessing a similar decline of social regulation, evident in the decline of norms, taboos, and in the almost complete disappearance of ideas of sin and guilt attached to sex. Does this mean that sexual activity, just as economic activity, will be more and more shaped by the laws of the market?

OVER TO YOU

Examine the advice columns of magazines where people write concerning sexual experience, or look at the 'partner wanted' columns of your local newspaper. What sorts of themes are present? Are the pessimists correct, and sexuality has been de-eroticised? To what extent does sexuality represent a search for an encounter with the other, that in some way must break free from the increasing extent to which it is organised as a market?

Crime and society

Robbing the rich

By NIKKI BARROWCLOUGH

The hunched figure of a teenage boy slips between the cars parked in one of the ritzier neighbourhoods in Sydney's eastern suburbs. It's almost midnight on a week-night. And the street is empty. On any other occasion a Porsche would do—he started stealing them when he was 14.

He's 18 now, and better at car chases, although he smiles at the memory of the Porsche they left rammed through the plate glass doors of a duty-free store.

He remembers the explosions as great shards of glass hit the pavement, the crunch of the shattered glass fragments as the escape car pulled up, the maniacal energy of his fellow raiders, the ear splitting scream of the alarm . . . and then, in less than 40 seconds, they were gone. Swallowed up by the city. A great gaping hole left in the entrance of the still brilliantly lit store, as if a bomb had gone off.

The ram raiders get away only seconds before the police arrive, driving at dangerous speeds to a prearranged spot in Sydney's west. Sometimes they get paid in cash and heroin. Maybe some clothes get thrown in as well. Ram raiding on heroin or some other drug only adds to the powerful rush of adrenalin. 'You feel unbeatable. And plus, when you've got a good car and good driver, nothin' can stop you.'

Because of legal restraints and cases pending, the ram raid described above is a composite made up of real incidents, eye-witness accounts and actual dialogue used in an interview with three teenage boys facing charges including car

theft, robbery in company, dangerous driving and having goods in custody.

The boys are currently in detention at Mt Penang juvenile justice centre, just outside Gosford on the NSW central coast. One of the teenage boys gives himself the cartoonish-sounding name of Teddy Funklemeister. The other two youths are 18 and 17, and choose the pseudonyms Terry Olkas and Bill Olson.

There have been about 200 ram raids in Sydney since mid-1994, netting thieves millions of dollars. The police have claimed that the number of ram raids has dropped significantly.

The latest ram raid was in March this year. The target was Nitrogen, an upmarket store in George Street which sells expensive street fashion, with labels including Ralph Lauren Polo Sport, Boss and DKNY.

Four masked men reversed the current ram-raiding car of choice, a Subaru Impreza WRX, through the front of the store, and hurled $30,000 worth of clothing in the car and were gone within 30 seconds.

There's plenty of demand for the kind of designer merchandise the ram raiders steal. In Sydney, the pursuit of image and hunger for life in the designer label fast lane has fostered a voracious appetite. And while we may safely assume that the 'rich' and the ram raiders do not know each other socially—even if the line between high society and heist society is not always clear in a city like Sydney—their love of designer desirables gives them something in common.

One difference between the two groups is the way they go about making the money to buy the clothes, watches, sportswear and jewellery that spell the kind of image that 'everyone' wants. The rich are followed around by tax-lawyers, ram raiders by the smell of burning rubber.

Funklemeister, asked about the motives of teenagers who think nothing of leaving a Porsche jammed in the doors of a duty-free store, replies: 'It's not about being better than anyone else. It's about getting for yourself. It's about having.'

Of the Castlereagh Street targets, he says, 'It's like they're rich, but they're not losing anything.' 'Thieves coming to collect,' grins Olson.

What do the ram raiders do with the money? 'It depends,' says Funklemeister. 'If they need clothes, they go and buy clothes that fit them. If they need shoes, they need shoes. That's what it's about,' he repeats. 'Because it all turns into money.'

Olkas points out that it's important to look good. 'You don't want to go out lookin' like bums, or nuthin'. You wanna dress nice.'

'You want to keep up with the trends,' adds Funklemeister, of his peer group in general. 'You want the clothes, you want the shoes, you want the jewellery.'

In his recently published book, *Danziger's Britain: A Journey to the Edge*, author Nick Danziger writes: 'I found that Britain was becoming more homogeneous . . . Because of the proliferation of the many tentacles of the media which were ▶

dedicating people's minds to one goal—consumption . . . Young people looking for an identity . . . can only find it through consumption: Nike trainers, Gore-Tex jackets, mountain bikes and drugs.'

Two years ago, an article in *The Sydney Morning Herald*, describing a teenage guest at an inner-city dance party, commented: 'The boy standing next to me on a pair of rollerblades has a TAG watch and is carrying a pair of suede Pumas (the cult running shoes), a mobile phone and a military inspired haircut. He isn't considered pretentious—just the quintessential middle-class raver.'

Olson, asked why he believes image is so important, looks startled, before replying: 'If I could answer that, I wouldn't need any of this. You wouldn't have to wear the best clothes. You'd just rock around like that bloke there'—he points at a tradesman walking towards the detention centre—'wearing a Hang Ten shirt or something.'

'Because we're young, we want the best, so we'll get the best,'

Olkas interrupts. 'If you see a girl and you're wearing bummy clothes, they won't even look at you.'

It seems pointless to ask them whether cynicism plays any part in juvenile delinquency in Australia, although criminologist Professor Paul Wilson of Bond University says in his experience 'there's an awareness of the Alan Bond, Christopher Skase phenomenon (among) young delinquents. They are also aware of (the difference) between the mobile phone set and themselves'.

He says that on the Gold Coast, where graffiti scrawled on the walls of the homes of the wealthy is an increasing phenomenon, 'you get road crimes, where young kids literally weave through the traffic and try to cut off wealthy cars'.

Wilson adds: 'My view has been for some time now that as the gap between the haves and the have-nots increases in Australia, it will become more acceptable for the have-nots to say, "To hell with it, we'll take from the haves."'

Don Weatherburn, director of the NSW Bureau of Crime Statistics, notes that 'in the overwhelming number of cases, the poor still rob the poor, which is one of the great paradoxes and tragedies,' he adds. The haves and the have-nots occasionally get their wires crossed, of course.

Funklemeister, Olkas and Olson say they do not envy wealthy people—'Good luck to them, they earned it'—but they want to have money as well.

'If it wasn't ram raids, it would be something else,' says Olkas. They agree that even more than the thrills and the adrenalin rush they keep talking about, money becomes the main addiction. 'It's like, you can never get enough money,' reflects Olson. 'Even if you get 30, 40, 50 grand, it's never enough.'

'No one saves, man,' they add. 'They might save six grand for a week, then it gets blown,' Olson shrugs.

Good Weekend
Sydney Morning Herald & The Age
19 April 1997

A day in court

By NICOLE BRADY

This is a tale of vice and human frailty. Greed and excess. Of heroin, violence, fear, booze, poverty, unlawful entry, theft, unemployment and gambling. It is the tale of Court One at the Dandenong Magistrates Court. It unfolds, Monday to Friday, day by day, week by week, a story without end.

The passing parade of stories at the Dandenong Magistrates on Monday would soften the hardest heart. Sure, the defendants appearing in Court One were pleading guilty to criminal acts, but each had

a troubled past. A sad story in the closet.

Dandenong has one of Melbourne's biggest and busiest magistrates courts. Each weekday, seven or eight magistrates sit in judgement. On average, it has 150 criminal matters listed each day. It processes the most family violence applications in the state—up to 50 a day.

As far as courts go, it is not a bad place. Almost new (it opened in August 1994), the building is clean and spacious, there is somewhere to go to have a cry, and private rooms where you can talk to your lawyer.

9.30am The car park is full. Battered Cortinas, Toyotas with P-plates, a silver Mercedes; a BMW bearing the sticker of a South Yarra car dealership is a long way from home. People gather on the court steps, many of them are smoking; most look sad.

Underground, in the police cells, Major Ted Gray, a Salvation Army officer, and two volunteers have been hard at it for an hour. There are 16 prisoners in the cells this morning; some have come from jail, others were picked up over the weekend. Major Gray has a kind ▶

word for all of them and is happy to telephone their families, organise clean clothes, or contact a Legal Aid solicitor.

At ground level, children are crying, people smelling of cigarette smoke queue at the information desk, while others hold hands and whisper in the waiting area. All around stride men and women in suits, talking loudly to each other and into mobile phones—these are solicitors and barristers, and this is their place.

10am It is quiet inside Court One. Police prosecutors, solicitors and the clerk share subdued laughter and tales of the weekend's adventures while strangers fumble for a place on the benches. A barrister tries to relax a client with a joke about some crimes still warranting immediate transportation to Tasmania.

The client does not laugh.

10.08am The young male clerk stands up and directs, 'All stand, please' as magistrate Christine Thornton enters the room. 'The first division of the Dandenong Court is now open. Please be seated.' An attractive, quite young woman, Thornton defies the judicial stereotype.

First up is an older man applying to shorten the time between drink-driving assessments. The law states twice-convicted drink-drivers (or those with readings higher than .15) must complete two courses 12 months apart, but this man is eligible to get his licence back in a few months and only did the first course last week. 'Why do you need your licence?' Thornton asks. 'I am a priest,' he replies. No problem, the assessment time is shortened.

Other applications for shortened assessment periods are approved. People sit slumped, shuffling their feet, then stiffen each time the clerk

calls a case. There is much coming and going: lawyers and police pause at the door to bow their head to the magistrate, others are more casual, dropping their heads as an afterthought.

10.20am A young father stands as his assault charge is read out. After hearing that the man is remorseful for a punch that broke a facial bone in a stranger's face and resulted in blurred vision, Thornton orders him to pay a $1000 fine within three months, without conviction.

Some drink-driving matters come next. Thornton chuckles at the case of a drink-driver with a blood-alcohol level of .078, whose excuse was that after waking with an upset stomach he drank a Scotch at 6am, a stubby of beer at 11am and then another stubby at 2.45pm—before being caught by police at 2.55pm.

'It's an old Italian remedy,' the lawyer explains. After hearing the man has completed a drink-driving course and shares a $270 pension with his invalid wife, Thornton fines him $300 and lets him keep his licence.

11.05am A middle-aged couple sit, heads bowed, as the prosecutor details their charges. The two plead guilty to forging a signature on a bank cheque to purchase $9879 of furniture and electrical goods.

This is a classic case of temptation. When a bank teller accidentally gave the woman a blank bank cheque, her husband advised her to throw it in the rubbish. But, six weeks later, there had been no inquiries from the bank about the cheque so the woman decided to use it and went shopping at a local furniture outlet.

Although opposed to the plan, the man hired a truck (using his real name) to transport the goods from

the store to their new Lilydale home. The bank, realising the cheque was not legitimate, refused to honour it and the store easily traced the couple via the truck's registration.

Once detected, the couple returned most of the goods and paid for those they had given away as Christmas presents.

Dropping his voice, the lawyer outlines the couple's combined income and expenses, then explains the man lost two young children from a previous marriage in a housefire. Thornton fines the woman $600 without conviction, and the man $400 with a conviction—because he has a police record.

11.18am Young people in custody are brought forth by police one at a time. A red-headed girl is remanded in custody to appear another day. A young man is ushered in: looking good with close-cropped hair, open shirt and dark jacket, he is distracted by a woman in the front row. Mouthing words and pointing to a piece of paper in his jacket pocket, the pair communicate.

Thornton, busily typing into her computer, appears not to notice and remands him to appear at Frankston the next day. As he is led away the man turns and calls out, 'I love ya, babe, all right? Thanks for coming, kid.' Overcome, the young woman runs sobbing from the court, closely followed by a female friend.

A long-haired young man appears next. The hopelessness of his situation is that he wants to go to Odyssey House for drug rehabilitation but a bed will not be available for three weeks. He will have to wait in prison until Odyssey has room for him.

Nearby, the Court Network ▶

volunteers are busy. Tissues, tea, coffee, biscuits and advice are on hand. Run mainly by women volunteers, the network operates throughout the court system. Volunteers support people through their day in court, explain the process and make referrals to other community services.

A lot of their work is with domestic violence victims. 'People get so nervous coming here—a court is a very frightening place,' says Bonnie, who works every Tuesday. 'Often we'll go in with them and practically hold their hands.'

2.17pm Only a handful of people are waiting in Court One. The prosecutor drones through cases of unlawful possession of stolen gardening equipment, theft and drink-driving.

4.50pm By day's end, the buzz and adrenalin that characterised the morning has faded to lethargy. 'It's been busy today,' sighs the Court One clerk. The courtrooms are deserted, the foyer is littered with soft-drink cans, cigarette butts line the steps and the car park is virtually deserted. Soon the cleaners will move in to scrub the place up for the next day's madness. One thing is certain, the crime and violence and tears never stop.

The Age
27 February 1997

Questions

1. Robert Merton argues that the basis of crime is to be found in the social structure. Modern culture values success and wealth, but only gives a section of the population the possibility of achieving these goals. Those blocked will be under pressure to search for non-legal ways of achieving celebrated social goals. They can be understood as 'frustrated conformists'. To what extent do the ram raiders fit this model? In what ways do they vary from it?

2. What sorts of offences are people charged with at the Dandenong Court? Are there social patterns present?

3. Nikki Barrowclough argues that the rich are followed around by tax-lawyers, ram raiders by the smell of burning rubber. This suggests that these two groups are part of the same cultural world. Are they?

4. Both of these articles raise questions about the relationship between the 'haves' and the 'have-nots'. Most crime of the 'have-nots' is directed against other 'have-nots'. Why is this the case?

5. Is, as Paul Wilson suggests, an increasing proportion of the crime of the 'have-nots' beginning to be directed at the 'haves'? What are the implications of this situation?

6. What do the experiences of the ram raiders and those in Dandenong Court have to tell us about self-identity in the consumer society?

7. Most of the people charged in Dandenong Court are men. The only woman convicted was charged with forging a cheque. To what degree is this action, and the circumstances of the woman, typical of female crime?

OVER TO YOU

Your textbook offers a series of frameworks to make sense of crime. List the different crimes from these two articles. What do they tell us about contemporary society? Which sociological approach is the most helpful in making sense of them?

Faith and belief

The spiritual supermarket

By MADELEINE BUNTING

The decline of church-going Christianity has not led to a decline in belief. Vestiges of Christianity such as carols and cribs now jostle alongside neo-paganism, astrology, tarot cards, palmistry, self-help New Age therapies and transcendental meditation.

People still want a Christian wedding and perhaps a Christian baptism, but this nominal Christian membership is not going to stop them consulting clairvoyants, dabbling in meditation, being fascinated with the paranormal and consulting an astrologer.

Religious belief has become a DIY cocktail: a mixture of the sermon on the mount, a paternalistic Christian God, plus reincarnation, the stars, feng shui and a sort of pagan pantheism of transcendence in nature. Welcome to the spiritual supermarket. Each person builds his or her own mosaic of practice, belief and experience. A lapsed Catholic described his fascination with Tibetan Buddhism, how his wife is on her local parish council, why he is delighted that his children are attending a church primary school and how a Bon spiritual healer did wonders for his health (Bon is the Tibetan shamanistic religion that preceded the ninth-century arrival of Buddhism).

He rounded off his whistle stop tour of spirituality—he had a lot of time for Hare Krishna and was complaining that he could not find tapes of Tibetan Buddhist chants— by admitting that he baulked at being prescribed a deer's heart by his Bon healer.

We are moving towards a Japanese model. The Japanese people use Shinto, Buddhism or Christianity as they see fit: a typical pattern would be a Buddhist birth ritual followed by a Christian wedding—because of the white dress—and a Shinto funeral. This fluid interchangeability has provided the perfect culture in Japan for new religious movements to thrive.

Thousands of syncretic mixtures of religious traditions adapted for the late twentieth century have emerged, from the sinister Aum Shinrikyo to the wealthy and powerful Soka Gakkai or the Shinji Shumei Kai, now one of the world's major art collectors. Add all their membership totals together and you have a figure several times the population of Japan.

The up-market British magazine *Vogue* devotes pages to 'psychic chic' and prompts a flood of inquiries. The craze for feng shui— the Chinese art of arranging furniture and homes to promote health and wealth—has attracted clients such as the Body Shop, Marks and Spencer and the London soccer team Queens Park Rangers. This is not the preserve of the rich and trendy but is creeping into everybody's lives. An example is the success of 'The X-Files', the paranormal TV series.

Clairvoyants, psychics and astrologers are emerging from a subculture to a new respectability; people are no longer ashamed to admit they believe in communication with the dead or being influenced by their horoscopes. The most sane, ordinary people can turn out to be witches who organise

Sabbaths—in the nude—in their front room, or have devised their own rituals for births, deaths and marriages.

Born again Christians may claim a God-inspired revival but the spread of charismatic evangelism can be seen as another example of the emphasis on experience.

At the other end of the spectrum, the rave culture has a similar emphasis on offering an experience outside normal, everyday life. Ravers even use religious language; 'techno-shamans' facilitate the ravers being transported into communal ecstasy. Spirituality becomes a search for life-enhancing and life-transforming experiences that will make you a better person who can live more skilfully—calmer, more intuitive and more alert. The quest is for an internal spiritual balance or empowerment: self-perfection. As TV's Oprah Winfrey claims: 'I'm highly attuned to my divine self.'

Spirituality can become an aid to operating in the competitive market economy as a means to achieving your full individual potential. This explains why companies sign up their management for training courses that incorporate New Age self-help therapies.

The fascination with the future is a response to the unpredictability of the competitive market economy. Lives are much less predictable: there are fewer jobs available and no careers that promise security of life tenure. Your job depends on your ability to keep succeeding and to calculate risks. Even family and home life, once perceived as a refuge from the harshness, is ▶

riddled with uncertainties of whether marriages will last or parent—children relationships break down. Hence the desire for any clues of what the future might hold.

Is this the fertile ground in which dangerous cults such as Aum Shinrikyo, Waco and the Order of the Solar Temple could thrive? Some argue that a culture of credibility and suggestibility, in which people—particularly the young—are game to try anything, makes them

vulnerable. Other people differ. Some argue that the key characteristics of the spiritual supermarket are a suspicion of all authority and uncompromising individualism that are unlikely to make people susceptible to a cult's demands for loyalty and commitment. But there are clearly going to be quacks.

Perhaps we no longer believe in reason and science to be the engines of human progress, the promise of the Enlightenment; we

no longer believe in a communist paradise and, most recently, the glitter of the 80s' enterprise culture has gone tacky and tawdry.

The privatisation of religion prompts dire predictions, likening the fragmentation of belief in our culture to that which existed in the last years of the Roman Empire.

The Age
2 January 1997 (originally published in *The Guardian*)

The crisis of meaning

By JOHN CARROLL

In the West the humanist attempt to replace the religious view of the human condition with one centred on the individual has failed. The value placed on me and my pleasures, the material comforts provided by industrial civilisation, the scientific Darwinian picture of human evolution, have all served to undermine traditional beliefs without providing credible new answers to the age-old fundamental questions: Where do I come from, what should I do with my life, what happens to me at death?

Here should be a fertile social environment for a second Reformation, for a revitalised Christianity. Yet the churches seem to be becoming even more marginal to life in the Western world. It is time for a frank sociological reading of the contemporary position of the church, its confused sense of mission and the direction that new explorations of sacred possibility, of worship in the secular, appear to be taking in the West.

The Reformation picked up what would prove to be the central inward tendency of the West over the

next five centuries, a half-millennium at the end of which we stand.

The master account of this history remains Max Weber's book *The Protestant Ethic and the Spirit of Capitalism*. Above all, the Reformation took religion out of the monasteries and churches into everyday life. It did so through effecting two major shifts in belief.

Stress was put on conscience as the sole mediator between God and the individual. As much as the humanist movement had founded a new individualism, based on reason and free will, the Reformation initiated a contrasting one, based on the moral faculty in each person, with the power to instruct on how to live and what to do.

This view of conscience would become a staple of Western belief, one which would come to threaten the teaching authority of any social institution from the grand magisterium of the Catholic Church down to the concerns of parents within humble families.

The Reformation compromised the pre-eminence of the church in a second way, by separating the notion of vocation from its narrowly

religious tradition, bestowing sacred status on any work, however secular in form, from administering the Treasury to collecting garbage, as long as it was conducted in the right spirit—seriously, methodically, with devotion.

Here was the heart of the cultural revolution, overturning the traditional picture of work as drudgery, a low and profane necessity to be avoided. Work was revalued as something holy, a demonstration of a person's state of grace, central to the good life.

Amplifying this Reformation tendency was the relocation of the centre for community and worship outside the churches, and not only in the workplace. The home too and the affairs of public life became domains within which humans might exercise their higher calling.

The new Protestant ethos was vividly and poignantly evoked in the 17th century by Vermeer in paintings in which ordinary mundane activities and everyday objects are infused with a sacred glow.

While the 20th century has seen the steady decline in practised church Christianity, there has ▶

been little sign of a faltering in the force with which these two neo-Calvinist logics have driven through modern life. If anything the momentum is increasing to find a deeper engagement in the worldly—in the private and the intimate, in local groups, and in the natural environment, an engagement that is more than that of passing pleasure.

There are fairly clear signs of the direction to come. Some local churches, city cathedrals and other religious sites will remain to be used for marriages and funerals and as serene spaces individuals may visit for prayer and reflection. Here and there an unusual congregation will sustain its regular worship.

Meanwhile, some secular venues have been sacralised.

The most obvious are sporting arenas, in relation to which it is commonplace to hear such expressions as 'sacred turf', 'awesome play', 'sheer magic', 'a hush in the crowd', and see badges, scarves, other clothing in the colours and mementoes all valued as icons and certain players alluded to as gods. These arenas are new centres for weekly homage.

Such revaluations are not to be dismissed as sham religion. They occupy rather some intermediary ground between pure sacred and wholly secular.

At the same time, the main avenue of communal moral discourse has moved to television soap opera, talkback radio and newspaper opinion.

The home has retained its own quasi-sacred status as the 'haven in a heartless world' of sociological analysis. It is the sanctuary from the profanely public.

As the locus for old familiar objects and secure spaces, the favourite armchair and the ancestral fruit bowl, keeping the past alive while nurturing the future, it remains the enchanted hearth, however utilitarian and consumption-oriented its daily activity. It is the place in which petty, mundane tasks are occasionally illuminated with transcendental significance and the overall complexion of life may find order.

The gravest problem in the modern West is the crisis of meaning. We have lost our traditional answers, without having found new ones, to the age-old fundamental questions: Where do I come from, what should I do with my life, what happens to me at death?

Intimations of grace may be found in secular life, in sporting arenas, in the home, in the natural world. Yet they will remain uncertain without an overarching theology or metaphysics, a credible picture of the whole.

The Age
19–20 June 1996

Questions

1. What sociological explanations might explain why clairvoyants are gaining respectability?

2. Functionalist sociologists link the expansion of cults and DIY religions to the decline of older forms of social integration and identification: work, class, kinship and neighbourhood. Should the decline of older forms of social integration be linked to the expansion of new religions in this way?

3. Western societies are increasingly fascinated by possibilities of alien encounters and UFOs, evident in the popularity of TV series like 'The X-Files' or the events in 1997 when cult members suicided in order to rendezvous with a space ship believed to be following the Hale-Bopp comet. Have aliens and a fascination with 'The X-Files' world come to occupy the place in Western culture once occupied by religions?

4. Sects are powerful social experiences which structure the world in terms of pure and impure, good and evil, and are organised in terms of hierarchy. Are we increasingly vulnerable to sects? If so, what sociological explanations can we offer?

5. Do Western societies confront a crisis of belief—no longer placing faith in science or social utopias? John Carroll argues that the gravest problem confronting the modern West is a crisis of meaning. Does it matter?

OVER TO YOU

Contemporary culture is increasingly shaped by quasi-religious experiences, from the homage of the football star to the fusional experience of the raver. Can we say anything about the cultural meaning of these experiences? Interview a group involved in one of these experiences—what themes emerge? What are the implications for sociological approaches to religious experience?

17 Ethnicity—imposed

Zero tolerance

By ADELE HORIN

The boys are no angels. Everyone says so, even their mothers. The boys themselves admit to a no-good past. They have stolen cars, wallets and countless mobile phones and a couple have served a few months in juvenile detention centres for armed robbery.

But now they are attracting a string of fines and charges of a different nature: $200 for jaywalking, $200 for throwing a cigarette butt, $100 for failure to wear a bike helmet. One was charged for wearing a baseball cap with the logo, 'F--- the Police', the name of a song by the American rap group Niggaz With Attitude.

On the Riverwood Housing Department estate in south-west Sydney, near Bankstown, the local police are cracking down hard on a number of Lebanese/Australian teenage boys for the most minor infractions: car defects, fare evasions, stealing a lolly. When they protest, the youths can cop a trifecta of other charges—indecent language, resisting arrest and assault of a police officer.

'We can't walk two steps without a police car pulling us over and searching us,' says Raymond*, 15.

The boys claim police harassment, racism and provocation. They are angry and frustrated and talk of revenge. 'It has the potential to blow up,' says Pauline Gallagher, co-ordinator of the estate's community centre.

In the US it is called 'zero tolerance' policing. If the police take care of the little crimes, goes the theory, the big crimes take care of themselves. Nab men for drinking

beer on the footpath and you will stop them from urinating in gutters, yelling late at night, fighting and even killing each other. Clamp down on uncivil behaviour and you can reduce the murder rate. It's the criminologists' version of the multiplier effect.

Whatever it is called, the police crackdown at Riverwood bears the hallmark of a zero tolerance approach. A core group of about 15 boys, many Australian-born but of Arabic-speaking background, is feeling the heat of constant surveillance, questioning, fines and minor charges. 'I used to steal cars, all right?' says Sam*, 17. 'Now I got myself a licence, bought myself a car, I registered it, I tried to do the right thing.'

But Sam's attempt at going straight failed to impress the police, who checked the car for defects and tried to search it for stolen goods. And recently, when a group of his friends were helping to fix the engine, Sam copped a fine for illegally parking over the gutter of the estate.

'Everyone does it,' Sam says. 'But they are always harassing us, bringing up our past. They look at us as criminals not as changed persons.'

The mothers of some of the boys also believe the police have gone too far. Two of them, in separate interviews, told of how they used to co-operate with the police for the sake of the whole community.

Rana Khalil* once found a mobile phone in her son's bedroom and took it to the Riverwood police. She asked them to search her son's room for other stolen goods. Three

police cars and six officers descended on her home. They found nothing. Two weeks later, uninvited, the police came with a search warrant and went through the house again.

'They pulled everything out, they found nothing, they apologised but it was too late,' says Khalil, through an interpreter. 'They have turned against me and my family.'

One of her sons has a string of fines for wearing the offending baseball cap, for jaywalking and for littering. The other has a broken wrist after an altercation with police which is now the subject of a complaint to the Ombudsman's Office.

Another mother, Samia Ibrahim*, turned against the police after about 10 police cars, some from the Kingsgrove and Menai stations, surrounded her elder son who was on foot, and arrested him for outstanding warrants. The response, she believes, was totally out of proportion. Half of Riverwood saw the scene and now she can't show her face.

'I trusted the police, I really wanted to help for the sake of the community,' says Ibrahim, 'but now they have stabbed me.'

On the Riverwood Estate, about 3,300 people live in shabby three storey blocks of flats and Redfern-style high-rise crammed over a few hectares. The estate is one of Sydney's oldest, beginning life as an army hospital in the Second World War. It looks its age, down-at-heel and cut off from surrounding suburbs.

But it was once a good place ▶

to raise children, says Pauline Gallagher, who lived there for four years in the 1970s and has come back to run the well-appointed and busy community centre.

'When I lived there, all my friends were in work. That is the different thing today.' It goes without saying that the boys at the centre of the current furore are unemployed and out of school. No local school will take 15–year-old Raymond after he raised a chair threateningly at a teacher. The Department of School Education has abandoned him to his fate. Another high school refused to admit Sam after he had spent two months in Mt Penang Detention Centre.

One boy found casual work on the council recycling truck before being retrenched; another does some welding work. A third did a panel beating course but could find no apprenticeship. With virtually no full-time jobs for teenagers, their future looks bleak.

In the past, even unskilled teenagers found work and often moved off the estate. Or, as the children grew bigger, the then Housing Commission moved families from the flats to houses in other areas. Now teenage boys hang around the estate, bored and idle. Even to participate in organised sport costs money their families don't have.

The teenagers live with parents and siblings in shoe-box flats long after they have outgrown the bunk beds and minuscule lounge rooms. The Housing Department has no excess houses to move people into these days.

While zero tolerance is the new fashion in international policing, its critics question its effectiveness.

'The big problem is that kind of aggressive policing is likely to antagonise communities,' says David Dixon, an Associate Professor in criminology at the University of NSW. 'I saw what happened in England in the early 1980s when police did very heavy stop-and-searches on young black people . . . Serious public disorder.'

'The more the boys are picked on by the police, the more they rebel, the more their future goes down the drain,' says Ibrahim.

Given the ethnic composition, charges of police racism are common. Waving his heavily bandaged broken wrist, Sam gives his version of a fight with the police after they allegedly told him to 'go back to your f---ing country'.

His brother was in the paddy wagon at the time, his mother was crying, and he claims he saw a policewoman laughing at her. He swore at the policewoman and was jumped on by a number of officers. Then he was charged with resisting arrest.

As the charges, the fines, the trips to the police station and court rise inexorably, so too do the boys' anger, and the mothers' despair. Says Pauline Gallagher: 'There's a siege mentality.'

When the police can't pin big charges on the youths, they have struck out in frustration with pettier ones. When there was trouble at the local railway station with purse-snatching, they issued the youths with notices for failure to have a train ticket. 'It's the only action we can take and we take it,' says Perkins.

*Names changed.

Sydney Morning Herald
27 March 1997

Questions

1. The Riverwood experience raises the question of the meaning of ethnicity. *Ethnicity* is an identity that social actors may claim as their own, a resource that is mobilised to make political or cultural claims, or as an experience of tradition or memory through which they construct identity. But ethnicity can also be imposed upon a group—one of the clearest examples being the Jewish experience in Nazi Germany where a largely assimilated group was 'ethnicised' and 'racialised', pushed out of the mainstream and into ghettos in an attempted genocide. The young people in Riverwood have an ethnic identity—is it one that is claimed as a resource to mobilise, or an experience of ethnicity that is imposed?

2. Sociologists like Howard Becker argue that identities are a product of a transaction or *interaction*. What sorts of interaction are occurring here, and what sorts of identities are being imposed?

3. Becker introduces the idea of 'deviant career', where a label, once attached, comes to shape the experience of an individual or group across a range of areas. Do we have a case of 'deviant career' here, where identity imposed in the suburb contaminates other areas, such as the school? How does this happen?

4. Sociologists of deviance argue that we all commit crimes, but only certain people are likely to be labelled as criminals. What are the

crimes that are being policed with 'zero tolerance' in Riverwood, and are these actions generally shared by the population as a whole? Is everybody policed in this way? If not, why not?

5. What does this experience suggest about the relationship between ethnic identity and social class?

OVER TO YOU

The Riverwood experience raises pressing questions about identities, stereotypes, and profile-based policing. It points to the possibility of excluded communities emerging in Australian cities, in which public services and housing are withdrawn, and policing is increasingly seen as the solution to social problems.

This experience may also highlight the declining capacity of some communities to regulate their own experience. As unemployment and the immigration experience weaken the authority of parents, they are becoming more dependent on the professional intervention of police and social workers to tackle the issues they are unable to deal with.

These themes converge in the relationship between young people and their community on the one hand, and with public space and the police on the other. This is a difficult area to explore through fieldwork, but one that is of increasing urgency in contemporary Australia.

One way to explore this issue is to interview young people over fifteen years old, perhaps meeting through local council youth services, and comparing two quite different suburbs—one affluent and the other more like the Riverwood experience. Ask the young people to talk about their experience of public places, and their encounters with police, as well as their relationship with parents. See if it is possible to interview parents as well. Make sure that you have *informed consent*, and that you are aware of what is involved.

Write up a fieldwork report that considers the following questions: Is there evidence of different forms of policing in the two areas you are exploring? Are identities being imposed, in particular ethic identities? To what extent does this represent a shift from welfare services to police services as the basis of social cohesion? To what extent can policing patterns be understood in terms of the decline of traditional forms of community authority, such as that of parents? To what extent is the Riverwood experience an exceptional case, and to what extent does it capture contemporary Australian experience?

In the Riverwood text we have no information about the experience of young ethnic women. Make sure that you interview young women as well as men, and that you consider the question of gender in your report.

Ethnicity—claimed

Scarved scouts know the ropes

By HELEN PITT

A khaki Islamic head scarf and long dress was perhaps not quite what Sir Robert Baden-Powell had in mind for a uniform when he created the scouting movement for boys early this century.

But in suburban Arncliffe, Muslim girls are tying knots, lighting fires and promising to 'Lil Olla, Lil Olla, Lil Olla'—do their best in Arabic.

Every Saturday afternoon, the 60 Muslim girls and 50 boys of the Imam Mahdi Scout Group—Sydney's first Muslim Scout group—loop their neckerchief through a leather hapse (Arabic for woggle) and pledge allegiance to 'My God and the Queen of Australia'.

In a hall next to the Arncliffe Islamic mosque, they learn how to 'Be Prepared' for life in the bush, earn badges for crafts skills and they learn about the Muslim faith.

'We go camping and come back with mozzie bites all over us just like any Scout group,' said Mrs Zeinab Hammoud, the group's leader.

Yesterday, the group sang at the second Australian Muslim Women's Forum. More than 200 Muslim women from around Australia gathered at the University of NSW to mark the birth of Lady Fatima, the daughter of Muhammed, and to talk about the problems confronting Islamic women in contemporary Australian society.

Miss Feruzan Asgar, of the Al Zahra Muslim Women's Association, said the conference was focused on educating women about their rights as outlined in the Koran and Australian law.

'The forum is about educating Muslim women as well as educating the mainstream non-Muslim community, who often just hear the wrong stories about us,' Miss Asgar said.

Mrs Zeinab Soukie, a 29–year-old mother of five, said very often Islamic women were unjustly criticised for wearing head scarves.

'When I first started wearing a head scarf I was once sworn at by a man who didn't think I could speak English,' she said.

'Another man once told me when he sees an Islamic head scarf he thinks of terrorists or kidnappers—but we want everyone to know we wear head scarves in respect of our religion—that's all.'

Mrs Shifa Mustapha, the Brisbane-based editor of the Islamic magazine *Insight*, told the women that society here tended to undermine the role of Islamic mothers.

'There is no reason to assume the role of a secretary or a lawyer is more important than a good Islamic mother.'

Sydney Morning Herald
15 November 1995

Questions

1. All identities have two dimensions. They can be *imposed* upon social actors, as a form of stigma or label, a process explored by sociologists in terms of a deviant career. But they can also be *claimed* by social actors, part of an attempt not to assimilate into the global market and consumer society. What is important in the experience of identity described above?

2. Sociologists believed that with the development of modern society, ascribed identities such as ethnicity would give way to achieved identities, such as those defined by social class. It is increasingly clear, however, that new forms of identity are being claimed, constructing a sense of memory that does not reduce selfhood to consumer identity or class identity. Why are we witnessing more and more what is increasingly called 'identity politics'?

3. The case of the scout groups underlines the inventiveness of social actors. The scouts are an agent of social integration, with their rituals of loyalty to Queen and country. But far from being an agent of assimilation, the group of young Islamic girls is involved here in a way that seems to strengthen their identity. This might suggest that far from threatening social cohesion, ethnic identities can be mobilised by groups to participate in mainstream social organisations. How does this mode of ethnic experience compare to that of the Arabic boys in Riverwood, discussed in the previous section?

Over to you

Interview a group of people about the meanings of their ethnic experience. To what extent is this an imposed identity? To what extent is it claimed by the group—and why is it claimed? Is it defensive, or a mode of experience that they can mobilise to construct a sense of self to give coherence to experience?

Aboriginal experience

They trash houses, don't they?

By DEBRA JOPSON

You've heard the stories. Someone knows someone who lived near a house that was built for some Aborigines and they ripped out all the wood and burnt it and then the house was unliveable. It is true that a lot of Aboriginal housing is in a poor state—but there is another story about how it got that way.

In its landmark National Aboriginal and Torres Strait Islander Survey results, published this year based on 1994 research, the Australian Bureau of Statistics (ABS) paints the most complete picture so far of the conditions in which indigenous people live.

First, most do not own their own homes. Seven in ten indigenous households are rented, compared with just over one in four of all other households.

Second, there is a shortage of well-serviced houses. The Aboriginal and Torres Strait Islander Social Justice Commissioner, Mick Dodson, reported last week that two years ago, an estimated $3.1 billion was needed 'to cover the accumulated backlog of indigenous housing and infrastructure needed in rural, remote and urban areas'.

Third, the ABS reported that one in three indigenous people lived in dwellings 'reported as unsatisfactory', with children slightly more likely than adults to be living in such conditions.

It's a matter of not enough to go around. In a population that favours bigger families and is far younger than most other Australians (and thus constantly setting up new families), housing shortages lead to overcrowding.

Of the unsatisfactory dwellings occupied by one-third of the indigenous population, 61 per cent needed repair, 53 per cent required more bedrooms, 48 per cent required more living area and nearly 30 per cent had inadequate bathing facilities, the ABS reported.

In more than 5 per cent of NSW and 13 per cent of NT households, one utility—either a toilet, bathroom or shower, running water, electricity or gas—is missing.

In the four weeks before the survey, just over 9 per cent of households had been affected by a breakdown of utilities such as water supply or sewerage. Was this the fault of the occupants? Two authorities have found that it is due to poor materials and overcrowding.

An environmental health and design consultancy, Health Habitat, which studied the use of showers, taps and washing facilities in the Pitjantjatjara lands of South Australia, recently rebutted the myth that Aboriginal people did not look after the plumbing.

'The major cause of health hardware breakdown is not overuse or vandalism but rather poor initial construction,' they reported.

The ABS reported: 'As the number of occupants in a household increased, there was an increased likelihood of the dwelling being described as unsatisfactory. The problem was most apparent in rural areas, where nearly 50 per cent of dwellings with six or more occupants were considered unsatisfactory.'

And there is another culprit—poverty. As the ABS explained: 'Indigenous people, particularly those living in community housing, were generally paying quite a low proportion of their low incomes in rent in 1994 . . .

'Revenue from rent then becomes insufficient to enable repair and maintenance of houses and utilities which, because of their remoteness, may also be more costly to repair.'

There are bright spots. In Alice Springs, the Aboriginal-run Tangentyere Council has successfully housed hundreds, allowing people to design their own houses taking into account their family and cultural needs.

Closer to home, the Aboriginal asbestos miners in the northern NSW community of Baryulgil built their own houses with their own hands. These have had to be pulled down recently because of asbestos contamination. In this case, it was a mine that trashed their houses.

They drink too much

In its report *Health of Indigenous Australians*, the ABS found that a greater proportion of Aboriginal people than the rest of the population had never drunk alcohol in their lives.

'This was highest in the Northern Territory, where about 30 per cent of males and over 60 per cent of females said they had never drunk alcohol,' the bureau reported.

It also found that compared with the rest of the population, proportionately fewer Aborigines had consumed alcohol in the week before they were surveyed.

In a 1994 ABS study, more than 9 per cent of male and about 27 per cent of female indigenous people ▶

aged 18 and over reported never having drunk alcohol.

The only comparable survey of the entire population, the National Health Survey of 1989–90, found that 5 per cent of males and 13 per cent of females had never drunk alcohol.

People in both surveys were also asked if they had drunk alcohol in the previous week. Nearly half the Aboriginal men and less than one-third of the Aboriginal women said they had—a result that lagged behind the general population in fondness for booze. In the NHS survey, almost three quarters of the men and about half the women had drunk in the previous week.

Yet indigenous people themselves see the grog as a problem. The ABS found that six out of 10 indigenous Australians over 12 years of age named it as one of the main health problems in their local area.

According to Norm Newlin, a drug and alcohol worker at Long Bay Jail, fewer Aborigines drink, but some guzzle their way to devastation—and part of the reason is prohibition, which in NSW was lifted only in 1963.

'It was illegal for Aboriginal people to drink, so people would throw the cork away and get it into them as quickly as possible so it couldn't be taken away,' he says.

Why are these drunks more visible than others? Because many Aborigines like to be outdoors. Because 'dress rules' and racism may keep them out of bars.

They don't want to work

Indigenous people are the only group in Australia to work for the dole, under the Community Development Employment Program. More than 27,000 people are paid the equivalent of unemployment benefits to do work benefiting their communities, ranging from creating artworks to collecting garbage.

However, this year's Federal Budget cut any expansion to the scheme, so that ATSIC, which pays the workers out of its funds, cannot provide 2,500 extra jobs next financial year as planned.

In NSW, the ABS has reported an indigenous jobless rate of 46 per cent. It has also found that the mean annual income for NSW Aborigines was $14,721, with 11 per cent getting no income.

The historians Richard Broome and Heather Goodall have written of successful indigenous agricultural enterprises at Poonindie and Raukkan in South Australia, Coranderrk in Victoria and Cummeragunja in NSW late last century. All were eventually thwarted by land grabs and government policies.

They get special treatment

'Special' funding is aimed at addressing indigenous disadvantage. Lois O'Donoghue, the former chairwoman of the Aboriginal and Torres Strait Islander Commission, has pointed out that the diesel fuel rebate scheme, which favours farmers and miners, last year cost taxpayers more than the main vehicle of indigenous funding, ATSIC.

Yet ATSIC has responsibility for building houses and providing water, sewerage and electricity to communities that lack them because other government bodies do not provide them.

Aborigines claim special indigenous rights as 'first peoples'. They have also had a separate history imposed on them. In a survey of NSW indigenous people, the ABS found that about 8 per cent aged 25 and over had been taken from their natural family by a mission, the Government or welfare agencies.

Where their ancestors eight generations ago owned the entire State, the ABS found that 67 per cent in NSW do not own their own homes and are renting.

The descendants of the people who owned the country once described by the World Bank as the world's richest, when unexploited natural resources are taken into account, have been stripped of their economic base.

Yet NSW Aborigines have held onto their culture. The ABS found that in the past year, 67 per cent had attended at least one indigenous cultural activity, 82 per cent aged over 13 said the role of elders was important and 48 per cent identified with a clan, tribal or language group.

Most of them aren't real Aborigines, anyway

'If you are a child of a mixed race . . . you are a mongrel,' said Peter Davis, the Mayor of Port Lincoln.

The concept of the 'mongrel' person, according to Professor Colin Tatz of Macquarie University's Centre for Comparative Genocide Studies, comes from Count de Gobineau, a 19th-century 'French dandy' who wrote *On the Essential Inequality of the Human Races*.

He argued that previously, humanity had consisted of a long line of mongrels, but in the French nobility (that is, himself) finally a 'pure' race had emerged. These ideas were eventually taken up by Hitler.

'A "pure race" is pure mythology. There is no such thing on this earth. No race has been without inter-marriage,' says Tatz.

Everyone, as a result, is a mongrel. The Mayor of Port Lincoln, declares Tatz, is 'indubitably a mongrel'.   ▶

According to Tatz, when modern-day Australians speak of mixtures of racial blood, they are harking back to 19th-century 'so-called scientific racism', which tried to put the world's various races into a hierarchy—with Europeans at the top.

'Blood' has a nasty history in Australia. Tatz has written of the ludicrous official practice of trying to define the amount of Aboriginal 'blood' a person had. For purposes of allocating them to reserves or deciding whether to take them from their families, for instance, people were classed as 'full-bloods' or 'half-castes', 'quadroons' or even 'octoroons'. Some people still think that the only 'real' Aborigines are dark and live in remote communities. They claim that lighter-skinned urban Aborigines are not really Aborigines at all.

However, Jack Beetson, the studies director at Tranby Aboriginal College—who as a light-skinned kid in Nyngan in the 1960s hid from the 'welfare'—points out that even 'white' Aborigines, by dint of their association with the community, have still often been racially vilified, relegated to the bottom of the class and over-policed.

'There is the argument that some fair-skinned "Johnny come latelies" are in it for the money,' says Aaron Ross, the NSW State public affairs manager for the Aboriginal and Torres Strait Islander Commission.

'Why go through the bother of being questioned by your own mob and non-Aboriginal people about your identity? It just isn't worth the limited benefits available to you—if there are any at the end of the day.'

Sydney Morning Herald
19 December 1996

Questions

1. The Australian Bureau of Statistics and other organisations have researched the reasons for poor Aboriginal housing in Australia. What conclusions do they draw?

2. Cultures develop ways of regulating alcohol consumption through traditions and norms. It is suggested that this has not occurred in Aboriginal culture. Why not?

3. The ABS concludes that 1 in 12 Aboriginal people in New South Wales above the age of 25 was removed from their parents. Why was this done?

4. Has the Aboriginal population been assimilated, or does the evidence suggest a continuation of cultural practices?

5. Where does the idea of 'race' come from, and are people 'pure' and 'impure' on the basis of race? Why were racial policies applied to the Aboriginal people?

Black search for meaning

By COLIN TATZ

When an Aboriginal lad died in police custody in the cotton-picking town of Wee Waa, New South Wales, the 'episode' stirred one of my students to write on what, rather than who, killed Eddie Murray.

Specific suspicions aside, the death seemed singular. Christine Stafford discovered that before Eddie's death in 1981, there were—across the country—fewer than 20 recorded Aboriginal suicides in police or prison care.

Aboriginal suicide barely rated a mention in the largely anthropological literature. Murray's death was therefore extraordinary: sinister we thought. By the time Lloyd Boney died at Brewarrina in 1987, the 16th death that year, Bob Hawke was prepared to listen to the Committee to Defend Black Rights.

The Royal Commission into Aboriginal Deaths in Custody, appointed in 1987, then inquired into 99 deaths between January 1980 and April 1991, concluding with 339 recommendations in five volumes.

Unexpectedly, perhaps, foul play didn't emerge; 37 per cent were from natural causes, 34 per cent were self-inflicted, 9 per cent were associated with substances, only 5 per cent resulted from custodians' ▶

actions, and the rest were occasioned by fights or accidents.

Aborigines die in custody at a rate relative to their proportion of the jail population. But they are grossly overrepresented in custody and 'too many Aboriginal people are in custody too often'. That, says the commission, is the crux.

Change called for includes the need for self-determination, improving the criminal justice system, breaking the cycle of youth unemployment and substance abuse, coping with alcohol, increasing economic opportunity, improving the obvious disasters of housing and health, and addressing land needs.

There were 19 black deaths in custody last year, despite the $400 million spent by Canberra on 'underlying issues'.

The slanging between federal and state governments, between governments and oppositions, resumed. The cry is for more money, for fewer arrests, for decriminalisation of certain offences. But is that where the answers lie?

The key issue isn't 'assisted death', as many thought.

It isn't simply suicide in custody, since the rate there is not disproportionate, as many thought. The catastrophe is not so much that Aboriginal youth are over-arrested, grim as that statistic is. The problem is not, as so many think, simply insufficient funds, lack of employment, housing, poor health, racist cops or the mix. There are many impoverished and oppressed societies in which, however ghastly the social environment, survival rather than self-destruction is the raison d'être.

In much of black Australia, suicide is no longer something alien, for which no Aboriginal language or dialect has a word. The human act of self-inflicted, self-intentional cessation of life has become a daily pattern—outside of custody. A suicide rate that was among the lowest has become among the world's highest in a little more than 25 years.

That is a record of some sort. It is also a stark indictment—not so much of our good- or ill-will as our inability to see beyond our diagnostic tools.

We see poverty, ill-health, racism in institutions and procedures; we have learnt something about identity, land, spirituality, traditional beliefs (and unlearnt much of it as fast as it took Hindmarsh to reach its 'conclusions').

We learnt a little from the commission, and some black and white historians, about the legacies of history and the consequences of such genocidal policies as the forced removal of children.

But are these factors involved in the teenage suicide and attempted suicide (parasuicide) that is rampant at Mornington Island, Yarrabah, Cherbourg, Mildura, Adelaide, Koonibba, the Kimberley? The works of Dr Ernest Hunter in the latter area, and of Dr Joe Reser in northern Queensland, attest to the cosmic rates of non-custodial suicide (400 per 100,000).

My own research (1989–94) revealed a pattern of daily parasuicides in all but 10 of 80 communities. Much of the behaviour was dismissed as 'silly' or 'attention-seeking'. However, girls swallowing Liquid Paper and thumb tacks demands attention.

Male suicide has now developed its own institutional and cultural roots, forms and idioms.

Two (of 13) types of suicide are particularly relevant. First, chronic suicide, the masking of a death-wish by the excessive use of alcohol or drugs. Second, existential suicide, the ending of the unending burden of hypocrisy, the meaninglessness of life, the lack of motivation to continue to exist—what the concentration camp survivor Victor Frankl calls 'purposelessness in all things', especially in future things.

Welfare funds, housing and jobs don't necessarily produce an inner sense of meaning. The oppressive and paternalistic mission and government settlement structures have gone. But so too has much of the reign of social and traditional law, of belief and loyalty systems, of kinship and reciprocity systems, of incest prohibition, of what used to be the best child-rearing and extended family system on earth.

Many communities are not really communities. The social cement has crumbled. Societies have become disordered, and in that milieu, traditional values—of affection, care, respect—have disappeared, replaced by maiming and killing others or self.

What can restore coherence, centrality in their lives? I advocate sport, an activity now proven to lessen violence, delinquency, lawbreaking (and need for custody). Problem: one cannot play sport, belong to a team, an identity, a chauvinism, a set of rituals that bind, for 365 days a year.

An enduring answer may be the example of Islam in black America, a movement that did more to bring coherence and pride to Afro-Americans than all the millions spent in health, education and welfare.

I think Aboriginal redemption may be found somewhere between such a fundamentalist religion and a radical political movement.

Colin Tatz is professor of politics at Macquarie University.

The Age
5 January 1996

Questions

1. Colin Tatz emphasises the breakdown of community structures and *norms*—from parenting, incest prohibition, to the motivation of people. Why would the experience of dispossession break down structures of authority in this way?

2. Tatz argues that social coherence and identity are linked to the coherence of individual experience and identity. Why does he argue this?

3. Tatz is using sociological concepts of disorganisation and *anomie* to attempt to make sense of the Aboriginal experience. What do these concepts mean? How might they help us to understand the contemporary Aboriginal experience?

4. How can we interpret the rise of a 'culture of suicide' that Tatz argues exists among the Aboriginal people?

5. Tatz believes that welfare alone is not the solution to this situation. What is he calling for, and why?

OVER TO YOU

In Australia we are witnessing an Aboriginal cultural renaissance, involving music, art and theatre. What themes are involved? See if it is possible to invite a representative of an Aboriginal group to come to a class to talk about their activities. To what extent does this point to an Aboriginal social movement?

20 ▌ Racism

Revealed—racism's ugly rise

By CAROLINE MILBURN and BEN MITCHELL

Signs are emerging of a steady deterioration in Australia's race relations, with experts warning that the nation faces growing social unrest and racial division.

New research has revealed that racist attitudes and remarks are widespread in Australian schools, as much between ethnic groups as from those of English-speaking backgrounds . . .

One race-relations expert, Professor Stephen Castles, of Wollongong University, warned that Australia faced outbreaks of urban conflict in areas where unemployment and migrant numbers were high.

Studies of migrant students at primary and secondary levels by Professor Des Cahill, of RMIT, show:

• Racist incidents are as much inter-ethnic as they are between students from English-speaking backgrounds and non-English speaking backgrounds.

• An emerging middle-class disquiet among Anglo-Australian parents as Asian children from business migrant families move into wealthier schools and surge to the top of the class.

• Some racist incidents are triggered by jealousy towards Asian students and their ability to study and achieve academically.

• Increasing tension brought on by the reluctance of students (particularly girls) from Asian and Middle Eastern families to participate in school sporting activities . . .

Professor Cahill said it was wrong to assume that most racist remarks and clashes were initiated by Anglo-Australian students.

Recent examples of racist incidents in Melbourne involved inter-ethnic clashes between students, such as fights between African and Asian students.

'We must not think that racism and prejudice only belongs to European cultures; the Vietnamese can be just as prejudiced against African students,' Professor Cahill said. 'There's a greater difficulty for Asian cultures to accept people who are racially very different, who are not European.' . . .

Another new study of attitudes towards migrants has revealed that Vietnamese people were frequently spat at in the street.

The Wollongong University study surveyed the attitudes and experiences of five different ethnic groups in Sydney's western suburbs.

More than half of the Vietnamese men and women said they were spat at while walking in the street . . .

The Age
2 September 1996

Study reveals anti-Asian bias

By CAROLINE MILBURN

Asian migrants were viewed with suspicion and hostility by Australians surveyed in a new study on racial attitudes.

Anglo-Australians living in the western suburbs of Sydney resented the influx of Asian migrants into the area, the Wollongong University study revealed.

There was a widespread but mistaken belief that Asians received government benefits not available to others. These included a car, a house and free loans from banks.

Yet banks and governments did not provide such things.

The study canvassed the attitudes of 150 people in five different ethnic groups living in Fairfield. The five groups were divided into ethnic origin—Anglo-Australians, Vietnamese, Italians, Iranians and Chileans.

The study's author, Dr Ellie Vasta, said the Anglo-Australians were overwhelmingly the most racist towards newly arrived immigrants, particularly towards Asians.

They were more tolerant of such longer established migrants as Italians and Greeks.

Hostility towards Asians was expressed by far fewer Italians, Iranians and Chileans surveyed. These groups generally supported multiculturalism, while most of the Anglo-Australians were wary of its benefits.

Dr Vasta said ignorance among Anglo-Australians concerning government services available to new migrants was very high.

'They will quickly tell you that ▶

Asian migrants get things free when it is just untrue,' he said.

Some people in the Anglo-Australian group believed it was easier for Asians to get jobs, which gave them an unfair advantage over others.

'On the one hand they were saying that Asians were taking their jobs,' Dr Vasta said. 'Yet they could not seem to make the connection that people with the highest rates of unemployment are the Vietnamese and people from the Middle East.'

She said most Anglo-Australians believed Asians did not share their values and did not understand what it meant to be an Australian citizen.

'But when you say that research showed that Asian people want to work, want Australia to be peaceful, want their children to do well at school, want to look after their families, they are surprised that the values are similar to theirs.'

Thirty people were in each ethnic group surveyed. Although the sample was not random, those interviewed lived in different parts of Fairfield.

Dr Vasta said racism towards new immigrants was more likely to occur in regions such as Fairfield, which had high unemployment rates and high migrant numbers.

Similar attitudes existed nationwide but were less likely to occur in the wealthier areas.

The Age
2 September 1996

Exploding the Myths about Newly-arrived Migrants

Myth	Reality
The Government gives a family a house and car shortly after they arrive in Australia.	Untrue. Families have to pay for such items themselves like any other Australian.
They get free or easy loans from banks, with government subsidies.	Untrue. Studies show that migrants find it harder to get loans from banks than other groups. No government subsidies available.
Migrants use more local government services than other groups.	Untrue. Anglo-Australians are more likely to use more local council services.

*Data collected in Fairfield, Sydney.

Questions

1. The rise of racism appears to be associated with increased levels of vulnerability, and with a way of constructing identity through rejection of the other—often on the grounds of myth. Why is this emerging as such a potent force in contemporary Australian society and culture?

2. To what extent is racism driven by economic vulnerability, and to what degree does it point to a pervasive identity crisis in contemporary culture?

3. Once social integration was assured by universal welfare programs and full employment. These are now undermined, and we are witnessing a decline in trust and weakening of participation in older forms of 'integrating' organisations—neighbourhoods, organised religion, trade unions, political parties. Do we step less and less outside our own communities? To what extent does this explain the rise of racism?

4. Is racism a mythical and ritualised way that we can exorcise our problems, focusing difficulties on a group which acts as a scapegoat? To what extent is the rise of racism linked not only to the decline of older forms of social integration, but also to the inability of the political system to deal with pressing social and cultural questions generating widespread insecurity?

OVER TO YOU

Interview groups of people in an attempt to understand the symbolic boundaries they use to construct their sense of self. Is racism an important part of their identity? Is race and ethnicity replacing class as the language of symbolic opposition and identity? What might be ways of overcoming this?

21 Globalisation

Global market mania—malign or benign?

By GEOFFREY BARKER

Fifteen years ago, in the glory days of free-market economic optimism, global financial deregulation was hailed as humanity's salvation from the inefficiencies of government and politics. Nowadays economic and social analysts debate whether, or to what extent, financial globalisation poses risks to Western economic and political stability.

Increasing numbers of economic policy-makers and social theorists see potential threats to the future of national sovereignty and representative democracy itself unless governments can find ways to control the volatility and speed of fast-growing foreign exchange markets. Within this concerned group there is a body of influential apocalyptic *fin-de-siècle* analysis that associates financial globalisation with political, economic and social disintegration that is widely perceived to be emerging throughout the Western world.

The disintegration is seen in growing middle-class and working-class insecurities caused by decline in manufacturing industries, intractable unemployment, widening gaps between rich and poor, and rootlessness among talented elites who prosper in the global economy due to their portable information and analytical skills.

Taken together, these issues make financial globalisation a major unresolved issue as the 20th century closes.

The election of the Hawke–Keating Labor governments ushered in Australia's headlong rush to financial deregulation through the 1980s. Sceptics were drowned out by barrackers for global financial markets. Yet today the secretary of the Campbell Committee which recommended financial deregulation in 1981, the distinguished economist Professor Fred Argy, is sufficiently troubled by financial globalisation to speak of the 'malign' influence of financial markets. He still believes financial markets are generally better at allocating capital resources than governments, but he says governments should stand up to markets more often than they have.

And Argy represents a decidedly middle-of-the-road view of the influence of financial globalisation on the long-term capacity of national governments to pursue sustained high unemployment and other social goals. Emeritus Professor Russell Mathews of the Australian National University argues financial globalisation has 'effectively put an end to the capacity of governments to implement policies which run counter to the beliefs of financial markets'.

He says government sovereignty over economic policy has been usurped by markets: 'The policy role of government has . . . been reduced to one of obedience to financial and foreign exchange markets,' he says. Emeritus Professor Fred Gruen, also of ANU, is more relaxed. He accepts that the growth of international capital movements has led to some loss of national sovereignty, but says governments still have a great deal of latitude: '. . . governments can make choices, but they also face the consequences of the choices they make—though the consequences now flow more quickly than before,' he has said.

Two questions arise: First, how far, if at all, has national sovereignty been usurped by financial screen jockeys pursuing quick global profits in liquid asset trading? Second, how much does it matter to national economic, social and political stability?

Neither question has a simple answer. It is clear that markets are perceived to be extremely powerful: all governments, with good reason, factor expected financial market reaction into the formulation of economic policy. Recent international statistics show the $1.3 trillion in daily foreign exchange transactions registered in 1995 has grown by 50 per cent since 1992 and by 30 per cent if the depreciation of the US$ is taken into account.

Moreover the editors of a new book, *The Tobin Tax: Coping with Financial Volatility* (OUP, 1996), note that 80 per cent of all transactions involve round trips of seven days or less—and more than 40 per cent take two days or less. 'More than short-term volatility, it is the instability and unpredictability of foreign exchange rates that make it harder and harder to manage national economies. Today's foreign exchange markets are beset with speculation and volatility, inflicting unnecessary costs—policy disruptions, resource loss, credit curtailments, production declines and unemployment,' they write.

But while financial markets complicate policy formulation, it is less clear where and when markets have punished or rewarded Australian ▶

governments for acting or not acting in ways approved by them. Fred Argy's point is that financial markets are ambivalent about governments that, for political and social reasons, seek to promote employment and economic growth by essentially Keynesian policies such as increased public spending, active labour market programs and monetary policies geared to growth as well as to inflation. 'Financial markets are saying if you want full employment, that's fine, but you have got to do it our way—deregulation, and tough fiscal and monetary policy. If there are still some vestiges of Keynesianism that you would like to pursue, perhaps adopting occasionally a fiscal policy that is sensitive to short-term unemployment, I think the financial markets would tell the government they had been bad boys,' Argy says.

Russell Mathews is much more trenchant. 'The control of economic policy has been handed over to gamblers,' he argues. Mathews's gloom is shared by the English economist and writer Will Hutton, author of *The State We're In*, and the late American social critic Christopher Lasch, author of the 1995 best-seller *The Revolt of the Elites*. Both associate financial globalisation with increasingly inequitable and unstable Western economies.

Hutton sees a process of marginalisation and social exclusion reproducing some of the worst features of the 19th century in terms of inequality and poverty. Lasch writes: 'In our time . . . age-old inequalities are beginning to reestablish themselves.' Writing in the American journal *Foreign Affairs*, Hutton calls for regulations to slow international financial transactions and to reduce their destabilising effects. He says free short-term movement of capital and floating exchange rates prevent countries from pursuing expansionary economic policies. 'Countries must recover the power to regulate capital flows and to manage exchange rates; finance must be compelled to behave in a more considered long-term fashion,' Hutton writes.

Lasch sees the late 20th century as a time where the world is at once more united than ever by the global market and more divided by tribal, ethnic and religious rivalries. 'The State can no longer contain ethnic conflicts, nor, on the other hand, can it contain the forces leading to globalisation.'

So far, the Australian Government has taken a relaxed attitude to financial globalisation. 'Globalisation has contributed to greater national wealth and therefore has raised the ability of the nation to fund social problems,' the Treasurer, Mr Peter Costello, told the *Australian Financial Review*.

There is no denying the destabilising potential of fast-moving money: the 1994 Mexican crisis was, for Hutton and many others, a glimpse of a frightening future. At present most governments seem to be adopting an Augustinian position: they desire virtue from financial markets, but are not ready yet to enforce it. What remains to be seen is how long they will delay action if rising social and economic insecurities start to further intensify global political volatility.

Australian Financial Review
25 November 1996

Questions

1. What does Geoffrey Barker mean by *globalisation*?

2. The article refers to processes of *marginalisation* and *social exclusion* accompanying globalisation. What do these terms mean? Provide examples of each one.

3. Barker argues that there is a widespread perception of economic, social and political disintegration in the Western world. How compelling is the evidence for this?

4. The older form of Keynesian welfare state secured social cohesion (social integration) through policies aimed at full employment and assimilation of different cultural groups.

Christopher Lasch argues that the late 20th century is more united by the global market than ever before, but increasingly divided by tribal, ethnic and religious rivalries. The state, he believes, can no longer contain ethnic conflicts. Are states being weakened 'from above' by global flows, and 'from below' by the assertion of ethnic, religious and racial identities? Does this matter?

5. Marx argues that the power of a capitalist class lies in their control of core resources and consequent ability to shape social transformation. Can the ways globalisation is being shaped be analysed in class terms?

6. Does the solution to the problems Barker is pointing to lie in a return to past models of social and national cohesion? Or are there potentially different social models of globalisation?

OVER TO YOU

As globalisation has developed, so too have populist movements throughout Western societies: from the National Front in France to the mobilisations around Pauline Hanson in Australia. These movements find their social base amongst groups who feel themselves socially, economically or culturally threatened by contemporary globalisation. Use a CD-ROM to draw together newspaper articles on such movements. What are their main themes? Are these forms of populism important, or a passing phase? What are their implications in terms of political culture?

Identity and the network society

Networks

By JUDITH BRETT

In his 1954 election policy speech, in the midst of John Howard's beloved 1950s, the then Prime Minister, Robert Menzies, said: 'We need workers with the hand, heart and head if we are to be a great nation.'

The image was of society as a body. Those who worked with hands, heart or head occupied stable social positions, as manual workers, wives (the heart workers) or educated professionals like himself. And like the different organs of the body, all were equally necessary for the health and progress of the whole.

This image of society as one of organic interdependence disguised relations of inequality and power between the organs. Those carrying out the functions of the head earned more money, had more power and suffered fewer injuries than the hands, who didn't get paid anywhere near as much and were far more liable to lose fingers. And many of those aproned heart workers were bored and resentful with their limited lives.

However, it was an image that did capture something of the stability of earlier social relations, and of the security many people found in an occupational identity that could last them a lifetime. No one thinks of society as a body any more. Today's dominant image of society is of a network, with the individual members all linked through myriad connections.

Have you noticed how many people talk of their social life in terms of networking? Or the excitement about the Internet as a new form of communication that allows people to log in as whomever they choose, adopting and discarding identities in a fluid free-for-all? As an image, the network is open, non-hierarchical, democratic even, carrying at its most optimistic a promise of equality and interdependence. Unlike the older image of society as a body, in which hands and head remained separate, in the network each point can theoretically link up with, or stand in for, any other point. It is the pattern of links between the points that is significant, not the identity of the points themselves.

And in the ideal network, the points will offer no resistance to the flows between them. All will be openness and exchange.

The network is a modern, technological image in which society is imagined in terms of a socially made system of communication. It is an image that carries all the confidence and optimism of humanity's capacity to transcend the barriers of time and space, of technology's power over nature. In contrast, the image of society as a body is modelled on a pre-existing natural form with clear, inherent natural limits.

The network is also an image much better suited to the changing experience of work, not only because many people in their work places now participate, through the wonders of computers, fax or e-mail, in the extended networks of information technology, but because of the way people are being forced to re-imagine their working lives.

No longer are people trained for specific tasks with which they will make life-long contributions to society's smooth functioning. Rather they are trained to be flexible, adaptable, multi-skilled, happy to re-train many times during their working lives, able to plug quickly into new networks. In the competition for work, communication or 'network skills' can be as or more important than any specific competencies.

But the network society has its down side. The identity of the individuals who make up its points can become blurred by the ceaseless flows of information, and only a few really relish the challenge to continually remake themselves. Most value stable friendships, both at work and home, as the basis of a secure, stable personal identity.

The down side of the image of society as a network is most apparent in one of its most dominant contemporary manifestations — the glorification of the market as an abstract and idealised system of exchange in which goods, services and capital flow freely between buyers and sellers with no regard for anything other than their mutual concern with the best deal.

'Market' is now more often used to describe abstract networks of exchange than the bustling, noisy bazaars of buyers and sellers from which the word is derived. In the ideal, abstract market, buyers and sellers are nothing other than points of exchange; they are not people with families, or histories, or futures, or national identities.

From the point of view of an abstract system of exchange, attempts by institutions such as ▶

governments, trade unions or residents' groups to regulate the workings of the market can easily be imagined as 'interference', like the unwelcome noise on an overseas telephone call.

John Howard harks back to the 1950s, to the security and stability of the social world in which dad was at work, mum was at home and the kids were at school. Yet he is an advocate of market-driven economic and industrial policies that promise to move society more towards the anomie and flux of the network than back to the security of the stable occupational identities of the 1950s.

Howard's continual emphasis on the family must partly be understood as an attempt to shore up the one source of stability left to many people as he kicks out the props that sustain their working lives.

Judith Brett teaches politics at La Trobe University.

An extended form of the argument is published in *Arena Magazine*, Issue 9, February–March 1994.

The Age
2 August 1996

Questions

1. Judith Brett points to a series of changes involved in the 'network society'. What are the main dimensions of this type of society?

2. Sociologically, occupational identities are those identities shaped by our place in a social system of work-roles. What are some examples of occupational identities that could 'last a lifetime'? Brett argues that these are weakening—is this the case, and if so, why?

3. The culture of chat-rooms on the Internet is one where identities are adopted and discarded, modes of self that individuals can explore in communication with others. Why are these 'virtual selves' increasingly part of contemporary culture?

4. What does it mean that 'only a few really relish the challenge of remaking themselves'? What are some forms that this challenge takes?

5. Brett argues that the constant flux of the network society may become *anomic*. The concept of anomie was developed by Durkheim. How did Durkheim use it, and what does it mean in the context Brett is exploring?

6. Brett suggests that the market is the dominant social expression of the emerging network society. Why is this? Could there be social expressions of networks other than the market?

OVER TO YOU

Interview people who are regular chat-room users. These are people who take pleasure in reinventing themselves, exploring their virtual selves. How can you characterise the form of freedom that they experience? Does the ability to be everyone bring with it the risk of being no-one, as stable identities give way to self-creation and the search for pleasure?

Virtual cities

Life forms in the virtual cities

By STEPHEN GRAHAM

How does the phenomenal growth of the Internet, the World Wide Web, and the new stirrings of virtual reality, affect the economy, social life and cultural activity of our cities?

Two scenarios compete. On the negative side, we might see the growth of the Internet and virtual reality to be part of a transition to a nightmarish *Blade Runner* scenario. Society is collapsing in communities riddled with violence, fear, crime, mistrust and widening gaps between rich and poor.

In this the Internet becomes woven into the vicious circle of forces that many argue are currently undermining the role of cities as public realms, within which all sectors of society mix in a free and democratic way. This is the view of people like Mike Davis, an urban critic in the US, who has starkly portrayed the collapse of public space in Los Angeles in his classic book, *City of Quartz*.

Broadly, the argument here is that people are exploring the Net because they are increasingly alienated by the processes of change underway in many American—and, by implication, other Western—cities.

The middle classes, for example, have scattered to be 'cocooned' in suburban areas which have little genuine public space aside from the carefully regulated spaces inside giant shopping malls.

Such (generally white) suburbanites are increasingly paranoid about crime and the incursions of different social groups.

Blacks, Hispanics and the poor attempting to enter these communities come under the scrutiny of police helicopters and 'armed response teams'.

This paranoia leads to gates and electronic surveillance systems being installed, which increases the isolation and fear. And so the cycle continues . . .

In British cities, too, these trends are noticeable. Many wealthy enclaves such as Hampstead in London, and Darras Hall near Newcastle, now pay for their own private policing.

In city centres, meanwhile, many public spaces where people used to mix more or less freely have been lost to redevelopment.

'Themed' heritage areas like South Street sea port in New York or Albert Dock in Liverpool have emerged. Vast, enclosed shopping malls, dominated by large retail and leisure multinationals, have been built over previously-public streets and squares.

Here, once again, many 'undesirable social groups' are purposefully excluded, often through the use of elaborate surveillance systems

Informal public space is squeezed out through commercialisation and people's behaviour is carefully controlled. Many new Disneyesque, privately controlled shopping areas in LA, for example, now forbid political demonstrations, 'loitering' and even sitting on public benches for periods longer than half an hour.

In this depressing context, Howard Rheingold, perhaps the most articulate US advocate of the power of 'virtual communities'

based on the Internet, suspects that 'one of the explanations for the (virtual community) phenomenon is the hunger for community of people around the world, as more and more informal public spaces disappear from our real lives'.

The Internet, in other words, with its informal 'electronic cafés' and specialised interactive discussion groups, is an electronic antidote to the depressing reality of contemporary urban life. It allows its dominant users—middle class, suburban—to keep in touch with carefully screened groups of similar people, right across the world, from the safety of their increasingly-fortified homes.

But while the unregulated and anarchic nature of the Internet may currently offer solace for alienated suburban Americans, some critics argue that it, too, is now becoming commercialised as one vast electronic shopping mall based on encrypted flows of digital cash.

Every large American cable, telecommunications, and media company is currently investing heavily in systems that will allow the Net to be taken over by electronic commerce. The dream is the consumer who spends at the touch of a button, at home. So, cyberspace might end up mirroring the narrow and commercialised orientation of most American malls and downtown areas. This antidote, in other words, might just be temporary.

Thankfully there is a more positive scenario. Here, the Net may help to bolster rather than destroy the democratic public realm of cities, so supporting a virtuous rather than a vicious circle. ▶

Municipal and local innovation in Internet-based 'virtual cities'—analogies to real cities on the Internet, which integrate access to all the web sites in a city—is seen in this scenario as a way of trying to reconnect the social and geographical fragments.

Distant suburbs and the diverse racial and social groups that now make up large cities might be brought together. The Net could generate a new public sphere supporting interaction, debate, new forms of democracy and new 'cyber cultures' that feed back to help support a renaissance in the urban, social and cultural life.

More than 2,000 virtual cities have now been developed right across the world which, as well as promoting their host cities for tourists, are trying to attempt just this.

In Britain there is now a virtual Nottingham, a virtual Liverpool, a virtual Manchester, a virtual Brighton, and many others.

In London, the London-Link initiative aims to connect electronically the public, private and voluntary sectors throughout the metropolis.

All the city web sites across the world are linked by the City.Net network on the World Wide Web, so you can explore them from anywhere.

But perhaps the most interesting virtual city is the Digitale Stad (DDS or 'digital city') in Amster-

dam. Originally set up for local elections, DDS has grown to be a very sophisticated virtual city supported with funds from Amsterdam City Council, the Ministries of Economic and Home Affairs and Dutch Telecom.

DDS defines itself as a 'test bed where the roots of electronic community can grow'. The most interesting point about DDS is that it provides a carefully planned set of virtual spaces intended to act as a powerful metaphor rebounding on to the development of Amsterdam.

The virtual spaces on DDS are constructed as a series of carefully iconised 'Town squares'—meeting points for people sharing the same interest in that particular theme (the book square, culture square etc).

Initiatives like the DDS are useful starting points for debate where the aim is to use the Net to feed back positively into the development of real cities. But we must be careful not to oversimplify the complex relations that seem likely to develop between virtual cities and the Net and real cities.

In developing virtual cities, public-access terminals and training for non-computer owners are critical. We must not forget that only a small minority of largely affluent, intensely mobile people are actually able to access the Internet at all and that 2 million households still don't even have a basic phone.

While municipal and local involvement in shaping cyberspace is

critical, such policies must also be realistic. Care must be taken to avoid being seduced by the glamour and hype surrounding cyberspace and virtual cities.

In fact, assuming that virtual cities can replace face-to-face contact may actually support the Blade Runner scenario rather than the more positive, democratic vision. As well as the stark unevenness in social access, relying on virtual cities may support a withdrawal of urban life on to the Net.

Useful Internet addresses

Following are useful sites on the World Wide Web for exploring virtual cities.

City.Net can be reached at http://www.city.net/. There is a useful 'virtual library' offering links on community IT networks at: http://earnet.gnn.com/wic/free.20.htm.

Useful material on the 'urban design' of virtual cities can be found at MIT Architecture and Planning School: http://alberti.mit.edu/arch/4.207/eadings.html.

De Digitale Stad, Amsterdam, is at: http://www.dds.nl/.

Stephen Graham is from the Centre for Urban Technology, Newcastle University, UK and can be e-mailed at s.d.n.graham@ncl.ac.uk.

The Age
14 May 1996

Questions

1. What does Stephen Graham mean by the *Blade Runner* scenario in terms of cities and their futures?

2. What do urban sociologists mean by public spaces? Why do they regard these as important? Are these being redefined as consumer spaces, with streets becoming privatised in shopping malls and suburbs becoming enclaves? Graham refers to British and American trends—what do you make of the Australian experience?

3. In many new Australian suburbs, the only shopping areas are shopping malls. In Western culture there has been a link between public spaces and democratic activity, such as the right to demonstrate or distribute political literature. Can you distribute political leaflets in shopping malls?

4. Graham refers to overseas examples of the Internet being used to bolster public culture. Are there Australian examples?

5. What are virtual cities?

OVER TO YOU

Visit a virtual city and undertake 'participant observation'. Also visit the web-sites of some activist groups associated with social movements. Graham argues that the relationship between virtual cities and real cities is complex. What do you conclude on the basis of your observation?

24 Postmodern community

End of the line—life, death and the Lilydale train

By SYBIL NOLAN

Billy Rowe was only 17 when he died trainsurfing on the Lilydale line. For many young people living in Melbourne's outer suburbs, trains have become the centre of their lives, a place to hang out, drink and surf. Sybil Nolan looks at train culture in Billy Rowe's world.

Friday night at the end of the Lilydale line. It's cold, and black and lonely up on the platform and once in a while, a group of teenage boys reeking of alcohol appear from the darkness and plop themselves unsteadily on a wooden bench to wait for the next train. In the country-town emptiness beyond the eastern end of the station, there are plenty of dark places where kids under 18 can go to drink, undetected by the police divvy van which patrols the car park.

The 10.22pm to Flinders Street is now departing. The 10 passengers are all riding for safety in the front carriage. Unfortunately for us, we're a captive audience for a troubled man who boards at Mooroolbark station and starts shouting incoherently in our faces. Still, it's a quiet night compared with some: just a few drunks lurching around Ringwood station when we disembark; a group of shiftless teenage boys drifting among the suits and shoppers arriving home late from the city; another five or six teenagers holding a drinks party on the platform. 'I wish you could have been on my train the other night,' a traindriver with 10 years experience tells me a few days later. 'I had a group get on. By the time I got to Lilydale, they had kicked out more than 15 windows.'

From Thursday to Saturday on late-night shifts, drivers on the Lilydale line lock themselves in their compartments, keeping an ear open for signs of distress in the carriage behind. 'It's like punishment having to do Saturday night,' the same driver says. 'You wouldn't go if you didn't have to.'

'You don't have families coming home from the city on Saturday nights anymore. It's sad,' says another driver, a veteran of 13 years.

A third recounts how, on a recent Thursday night, he picked up a 15–member graffiti gang at Mooroolbark and another one at Croydon. He could hear them fighting in the carriage behind him. There was just one other passenger on the train, a young woman with a pram, who got out as soon as she could. 'By the time we got to Ringwood it was an out and out riot,' he says.

Young people find the Lilydale line as stressful as anyone else. Chris, 18, who prefers not to catch the train at night, says there is a gang called 'CW' that operates around Croydon, doing graffiti and assaulting people.

'At Mooroolbark station, you see the same group of teenagers sitting, doing nothing,' says Rachel, 15. 'They all look at you as you go past.' Her friend, Chelsea, is 17 and has been out of school for a year. 'Ringwood station is full of idiots. I just don't like the people hanging around it. There's always scary people hanging around there.'

The girls and their friend, Zane, 16, agree that there are certain people on the trains you just don't look at if you want to avoid a confronta-

tion. 'As soon as you get off the train it's "I've got a gram, you want to buy it?",' Zane says.

The Lilydale line has a problem. You can see it even in daylight hours. From Croydon to Mooroolbark and on to Lilydale, where it terminates, the train line alternately winds through open space and a corridor of conventional 1970s and '80s homes.

Rich grass grows right up to the train line and there are large old trees in the backyards all along it. But it's as if a virus has run along the paling fences, withering the Morning Glory and carpeting the palings in a darkly riotous coat of paint and felt pen.

For kilometre after kilometre, the timber fenceline, the sides and backs of brick shops, the concrete underpasses and metal speed limit signs are covered in almost indecipherable scrawl that has been growing for years. In some places, the graffiti has been covered by fresh writing many, many times.

There is hardly a signal box that is not tag-infested, hardly a paling left bare. 'I have seen kids along this line spray-write on a pile of dirt. Now that's obsessive,' a railways employee says.

The Lilydale line, like many other train lines, is symbolic as well as a real fact of life in Melbourne's distant outer suburbs. For many kids who cannot yet drive or do not have cars, it is not only their lifeline, but their scene. They become involved in a train culture—a culture that can be characterised by vandalism, graffiti, and, in the most tragic cases, death.

Call it Trainland. It was Billy ▶

Rowe's world until he was killed trainsurfing one Friday night in early January. The 17–year-old youth struck his head on the Dorset Road overpass in Croydon while standing upright on top of a moving train.

The more you look into the case of Billy Rowe, the more it becomes a two-way window, looking out in one direction at the problems youth experience in the communities of outer eastern Melbourne, and back in the other direction at the problems outer eastern communities experience in their youth.

For many people out at Croydon, Billy Rowe is a vexed subject.

Some young people are still grieving over his death. Some fear unpleasant consequences if they speak out about him. Youth workers speak protectively about Billy, but to police and local retailers he was 'a potential problem' and had been interviewed by local police for other alleged offences in addition to those related to trains.

But Billy Rowe obviously represented something to the youth in the area. After his death, young people reportedly stood on the side of the train lines and shouted angrily at passing trains, as if somehow the train were to blame. At stations, some forced the doors open and shouted at the passengers.

Overnight, large pieces of commemorative graffiti appeared in the laneways and on shop walls around Croydon station: 'Rest in Peace Billy Rowe' and 'RIP Trigs' (his graffiti tag). That just about neutralised the $5500 graffiti clean-up that the local Chamber of Commerce had conducted in the shopping centre a few months before.

Visiting Croydon weeks later, it is impossible not to notice the contrast between the cheerful, tree-lined main street, and behind it, the graffiti-strewn car park abutting the railway station. Sometimes, first impressions are not misleading: it turns out that the latest annual police statistics show the suburb is part of a police district which has the second lowest general crime rate in Melbourne, but the largest number of train-related offences of any police district in Victoria.

The problem is the troubles of the Lilydale line are spilling over into the community.

A robust market town that was swallowed by the baby boom, Croydon, 26 kilometres east of the GPO, likes to think of itself as leafy and largely middle-class. In demographers' language, it is 'wealthy working class'.

'Of all the shopping centres I looked at (getting into), this one had a terrific feeling,' one Croydon retailer tells me. But he's shaking his head sadly on the morning we meet. In the past six weeks, the front door or window of his shop has been smashed three times.

Shopkeepers at the bottom of Lilydale's main street complain about harassment by train passengers, particularly young people, who disembark and loiter there. In a single weekend recently, 14 people, all under 20, were charged with carrying knives in public, and 12 with under-age drinking offences.

Those who live in the outer east will tell you that its clean, leafy environment is their region's defining characteristic.

But Dr David Hayward, an urban sociologist from Swinburne University of Technology, says that nevertheless, the region is a classic working-class, outer suburban area . . .

The Age
20 April 1996

Questions

1. The picture painted here is typical of all major Australian cities, but there are things happening that do not easily fit into older frameworks of community. These young people are commuters, and the train—Trainland—is their scene. Their community isn't a suburb, but a train line. Here it's the movement, not the destination, that counts. What does Trainland and the experience of youth as commuter tell us about contemporary youth identity and experience?

2. These young people subvert the functional logic of society—they sit still when everyone has somewhere to go, they occupy platforms during peak hour or block stairways. They step outside the functional logic governing movement and flow in contemporary society. Why congregate on a station rather than at someone's house? Are there themes of conflict, of symbolic opposition to the rhythms of industrial society, present here?

3. Billy Rowe died trainsurfing, part of a youth culture that seeks fame and intense experience, one where you hope to become a legend. There is no obvious correspondence between social class and trainsurfing. The issues at stake are more questions of culture, selfhood and the search for risk and recognition—themes also central to the graffiti writers who put their name or their tag on the walls adjoining the train line. Why is the search for recognition, fame and exploit so central to this culture—one that seems disconnected from generation and community as suburb, one that is always moving, but with no destination?

4. These suburbs are not ghettos, but were shaped by the expansion of the 1960s. They are centred on families and houses, but it is not sure that they can generate meaning and identity which young people can use to construct a sense of self and purpose. What does Trainland suggest about the sorts of urban cultures we need to develop in cities today? Is Trainland a new sort of postmodern place, one shaped by movement and flow more than by location and history?

OVER TO YOU

Plan an exercise in participant observation, travelling into Trainland.

What do you want to explore, and why? What do you need to know about observation techniques and ethics? Catch the train and write up a report.

Focus on the following:

- Does trainland represent a *postmodern* environment, defined more by flow and movement than by history and place?
- Consider the meanings of the train system. To what extent is it a symbol of modern rationality?
- Consider the ways in which you can sociologically interpret the 'commuter identity' of the young people you encounter in the text above. Their experience can be viewed as one of moving from place to place, but without a destination, of inhabiting environments which seem divorced from the meanings of place that are associated with suburbs. What does this tell us about the contemporary youth experience?

Subcultures

Wicked, what Generation-X thinks

By ALI GRIPPER and
ANDREW HORNERY

By 4 pm most afternoons in Beamish Street, the polluted strip which runs through Campsie in Sydney's south-west, most members of a local clique known as the Fijian Bula Boys have trooped into Lahoods, a dingy snooker room they often use as their unofficial headquarters.

Once inside, under the flickering fluorescent tubes, the Fijian Bula Boys, or FBB to 'brothers', tend to swagger as they walk. They don't usually like eye contact with strangers and they're not the easiest bunch to chat with.

'We prefer to wear Nikes,' 'Niko', 18, says calmly as he chalks his cue, his eyes narrowing into mailbox slits, 'so we can run fast between break 'n' enters'.

The FBB are not the only tribe to spray their graffiti tags on any of the area's available bus shelters and brick walls. Confuse them with their rival clans, the Sons of Samoa (SOS) of Belmore, or the United Tongan Boys (UTB) of Burwood, and they make it patently clear you could end up in one hell of a mess.

The FBB, the SOS and the UTB might sound like bizarre cliques but they are not peculiar to the streets of Sydney. You could find their 'brothers' wearing the same clothes and listening to the same music in the suburbs of Paris, Tokyo or New York, albeit under a different gang name.

Teenagers have always been attracted to tribes as a way of expressing identity but this is the first generation of young Australians to belong to 'global tribes'.

'They are the first generation to really experience the global village,' says Jeremy Nicholas, a youth researcher with Yann Campbell Hoare Wheeler market research. 'They are growing up with technology which keeps them totally up with global "spheres of influence", which have an impact in terms of clothing, music, attitudes and activity.'

Most of the FBB's identity, for example, is borrowed straight from one of the most dominant global youth subcultures known—the 'homeboys' or 'homies', based on black American street culture.

A recent report found that teenagers from countries as diverse as China, India, Canada and Costa Rica share common subcultures, based on globally syndicated television shows, movies, international pop stars, video games and transcontinental sporting heroes.

More than 10,000 teenagers around the world were interviewed for the Mojopartners research project, Teenmood. The responses showed that today's teens are more self-reliant than ever and are forming strong tribal groups to replace family structures.

Other global subcultures found on the streets of Sydney include grommets (young surfers), skaters, gothics, ravers (who dance all night to music styles they describe as Handbag House and Happy Hardcore), and the netheads—Internet surfers who drink a caffeine soft drink called Jolt to keep them hacking away into the wee hours.

Each clique is distinctly different, although some differences are more subtle than others and are not visually obvious. You almost need to learn a new language to understand them and the complex hierarchy of the global clans. It seems there is no such thing as the typical backyard-and-beach Australian teenager any more.

Ravers dismiss homies as aggressive fakes, because homies have borrowed their culture straight from the US. All you need to be a homeboy, ravers say, is a pair of droopy trousers, a pair of high-cut Nikes, a baseball cap and an interest in gang warfare.

However, the same could be said for ravers, who have taken their culture from English magazines such as *The Face*, which has been writing about raves for more than a decade.

FBB members such as 'Stash', 'Davey' and 'Missy' listen to hardcore rap which routinely chronicles drive-by shootings, drug abuse and other unpleasant realities of life in America's black urban ghettos.

Homegirl Missy says her idol is Snoop Doggy Dogg. She is probably unaware that the gangsta rapper was accused recently of murdering a 20–year-old gang member.

'They're called Generation-X,' says Nicholas, 'because there are so many influences and cultures that people gave up trying to explain what the next young generation is about.'

Young ravers wouldn't be seen dead in Campsie. They wouldn't last very long, at any rate, looking the way they do. A young female raver's usual get-up includes shiny body-hugging T-shirts with words like 'bitch' sprayed daringly ▶

across them. They usually go for micro skirts so micro they barely cover their bums.

In Sydney during the school holidays teenage ravers can be found at Fresh parties, legal raves organised in nightclubs for an 'over-15 audience'. At Fresh parties, as with most raves, teens have developed an inimitable dance style that can involve up to 5,000 teenagers jiggling up and down, not together, but in rows, facing revered DJs such as Pee Wee, Nick Fish or Jumping Jack. While the Fresh parties attract mostly white, private-school teenagers from Sydney's more affluent suburbs, ravers come from all socio-economic backgrounds.

'It's just a really good night,' says Andrew, 18, from Maroubra. 'People are really happy to see one another. It's not like going to a rock concert where there are people beating one another up and everyone's drunk. People go for the music and because they want to see one another.'

Andrew has been going to raves since his early teens and says there's a definite difference between a raver and homeboy. 'I've been to one of their parties out in the western suburbs and there were heaps of fights. That doesn't happen at raves I go to, because most of the people know one another.'

Dean van Dyke has been organising the Fresh parties since he was 15; a decade later the parties are still going strong. 'It's like going to a football match. It's a group thing. There is just so much energy in the room you feel good,' van Dyke says.

To the uninitiated, rave music sounds surprisingly similar to freeway traffic: loud, fast and repetitive, without a melody or chorus. To ravers, it sounds like a wardrobe of melodies from Garage and Handbag House to Trance, Trip Hop, Hip Hop, Hardcore and Happy Hardcore.

Dancing with another raver, face to face, would be so uncool you could be instantly exiled. Instead, they carry whistles, water bottles and lollipops onto the dance floor and gush about the 'BPM' or beats per minute of a particular track.

Ravers admit that drugs are part of their scene but most do not admit to having tried them. In this regard, they are opposed to the FBB homies who openly declare their taste for hard drugs.

Like most clans, you have to be invited to join, usually by an existing raver. At Fresh parties, prospective ravers have to lobby to be included on the 8,000-strong mailing list.

But for every hardcore clan member, there are thousands of young people who merely dabble and who are a lot closer to the teen mainstream. 'Most kids have a Nirvana and Mambo T-shirt, a pair of Nikes and a baseball cap in their cupboards,' says Nicholas. 'They mix it up, or dress grungey one day and then surfie the next.'

Simon Bookalill, the co-founder of the youth marketing company Spin Communications, says: 'If you were to dissect any high school in any part of the city you would have these groups there. In Campbelltown they have wax heads and skateboarders, hip hoppers and grunge kids.'

Waxheads and grommets, those young people who would rather search for the perfect left-hand reef break than turn up to a classroom or office at 9 am, have always formed a youth subculture which has defied the mainstream.

But there's a new breed at Maroubra these days. The 'Bra Boys' are the wild guys of the surf in Sydney, a tough crew who'd rather brave the stormwater outlet than be seen at 'Glamarama' a few headlands to the north.

The look in Maroubra this winter is T-shirts emblazoned with giant dope leaves or farting dogs. The Bra Boys wear Vans or Airwalk shoes, a kind of suede, thick-soled running shoe, and mirror wraparound sunglasses. They squash their salt-encrusted hair down under a beanie or a cap with PSA (Pure Surf Addiction) or SMP (Sex Money Power) written on it.

Some of them have the Maroubra postcode, 2035, or the Bra Boys tattooed on their backs or arms. 'If you're a real surfer you'll get into more grungey, home-grown gear than the big labels like Billabong, Rip Curl and Quiksilver,' says 'Jabs'.

Surf and sun hold about as much appeal as being burnt at the stake for Dawn and Brandy, two slender, corseted Newtown Goths. With their dyed-black hair, white skin, black eyes and swishy cloaks, Goths are one of the longest surviving subcultures.

The look is either deeply romantic (long velvet coats, crucifixes, corsets, medieval shoes, cassocks, all 18th-century ruffles and frills), or bondage gothic (lots of PVC and rubber, skulls, dog collars, body piercing and nose chains).

What sort of person is tempted into the fold? 'Someone who doesn't fit into normal society,' says Brandy. 'Goths tend to be thoughtful, literate and have strong politics.'

Goths see themselves as artistic, romantic souls needing to escape from mainstream culture. Brandy's Newtown Goth group discuss everything from Carl Jung and Piet Mondrian to the efficiency of their personal choice of hair dye.   ▶

'I spend about $100 a month on makeup,' says Brandy. 'Eye-liner, lipstick, pencils and a good foundation that doesn't make me look like a clown.'

They listen to '90s gothic and 'industrial' music: Nine Inch Nails, Frontline Assembly, Christian Death and The Wake.

Teens who surf the Net are generally seen as anti-social dags who can't communicate without the help of hardware. But now, says Stuart Ridley, the deputy editor of *internet.au* magazine, they have become the 'geek elite', regarded with awe by others who are not so technologically savvy.

'You can call us geeks, it's a compliment now, not an insult. But we prefer netheads,' says Stuart.

Netheads get involved in riveting e-mail workouts on Internet channels such as Rave or Quake, a kind of three-dimensional dungeon game. 'Sometimes you just lose track of time and the sun's coming up,' says Ridley.

Kathy Kondos, 15, loves sending cybersymbols like the face :-) to her friends on Channel Flower 'where everyone is nice'. Or she might post a 'flame mail' to her friends on Channel Hellas, the Internet chatting channel for Greeks stranded in the 'burbs and missing their home-

land. She also hangs about in Teen-chat, or Channel Sydney, reads *Wired* or *.net* magazine or the on-line Internet magazine, b0ing b0ing.

'Sometimes it's easier to say what you want to say on the Net than in person. All the physical triggers are gone and you can get to the heart of things more quickly,' says Kondos.

All her best friends are on the Net. They've hardly ever met in the flesh.

Sydney Morning Herald
26 August 1996

Questions

1. Early British sociological accounts of youth subcultures argued that they were constructed around the tension between generation and class. Young people were part of an emerging youth consumer culture, while also part of working-class communities. Later analyses argued that these cultures were leisure cultures, attempts by young people in increasingly deskilled work to define a domain, their leisure, over which they had power and autonomy. To what extent might these analyses help in understanding the cultures described by the authors of the article?

2. Chicago School sociologists argued that immigrant youth subcultures were defined by an 'in-between' experience. They were young people who were no longer part of traditional society and culture (which was often weakened or 'disorganised' as a result of the unemployment of the father), while they were excluded from participating in the new society as a result of exclusion at school or unemployment. Neither part of the old nor part of the new, these

young people construct forms of order and identity in worlds of disorder. Hence the hierarchical model of the gang experience, one which offers structure (loyalty, hierarchy and spatial boundaries) and identity (clothes, rituals and symbolic boundaries). To what extent do any of the subcultures described here correspond to this model?

3. For the functionalist tradition, youth cultures were a bridge between the family and the mainstream—youth cultures were a means to achieve social integration. These cultures are all part of global flows—are they an instrument of social or cultural visibility, or do they point to a segmentation of the youth world into non-communicating and non-intelligible 'tribes'?

4. Feminist sociologists argue that subcultures may allow young women to explore modes of female experience and to construct gender identities against dominant forms of femininity. To what extent is this present in rave and gothic cultures?

OVER TO YOU

Set out the main sociological approaches to subcultures, and explore the meanings of one subcultural experience in the light of the different analyses. Which is the most convincing approach, and why? Present your interpretations to your tutorial group.

26 Consumer capitalism

Retail times are a changin' — quickly

By KATHRYN HOUSE

Australia's retail market will be almost unrecognisable within two decades, shaped by new technologies, an ageing population and changing consumer needs.

That is the forecast of the country's major retailers and property investors, who, in a recent Byvan Management survey, said the Australian retail industry is changing faster than at any other time in the country's history.

Their outlook: even bigger regional centres with a strong leisure element; emerging strength in strip shop locations targeting the 'time poor' consumer; an influx of new international players; the death of many traditional specialty retailers; strong growth in the bulky goods sector; and a potential rise in electronic shopping.

In the recent Byvan survey, *Retail 2000*, Mr Kelleher said: 'The one certainty facing the retail industry is further change and a faster pace of change. In 20 years' time we will see a retail industry almost unrecognisable from that of today.'

'Retailers will over the next decade change from being property and inventory driven to supplying information. Retailers will collect information about suppliers, merchandise and customers and sell and network that information.'

For the shopping centre developer and owner, security would become a 'burning issue', as crime becomes more focused on shopping centres. And 'fantasy' would need to be injected into a centre if consumers were to be 'enticed into a shopping experience'—a trend already evident in the US where retail was linked to casinos, theme parks and film studios.

According to Mr Kelleher, the retail market will also diverge towards the upper and lower quality ranges, leaving mid-range retailers to shrink their store numbers or disappear.

Australian Financial Review
30 January 1997

Taking people's desires and selling them back

By ERIN KENNEDY

'The happiest place in the world' is how one visitor describes Disneyland in *The Tourist*. The programme looks at theme parks, simulator rides and journeys into virtual reality, and talks to a tutor at—believe it or not—Disney University, where 'cast members' are instructed in the rigid rules of how to treat visitors to Walt's kingdom.

Perhaps more unbelievable than Disneyland are some of the themed hotel environments springing up, such as those in Las Vegas which include reconstructions of some of the great monuments of ancient Egypt.

As author Dean McCannell puts it: 'The theme park is kind of the end point of consumer capitalism where you can take away the imagination, take away people's desires, and then sell them back to them.'

The Dominion
14 April 1997

Screams of terror turn to tears of joy at theme parks

By MICHAEL O'MEARA and SONIA SYVRET

Theme park owners and operators are on an exhilarating ride.

While many resorts struggle to make a commercial return from overcapitalised and under-performing resort properties, theme parks are rapidly increasing their assets and earnings.

So strong is the industry that operators in the Brisbane–Gold Coast corridor, where most of the country's parks are concentrated, are planning about $300 million in ▶

new developments this calendar year.

Dreamworld, in the middle of the corridor, has just spent $16 million building its latest attraction, the Tower of Terror, which opened last week. Punters pay $39 for the privilege of being accelerated to 160 km/h in seven seconds before rocketing, ashen-faced, up a 38–storey-high tower. They return to earth at a similar speed, spending about $6\frac{1}{2}$ seconds weightless on the way down. On a busy day they may have queued for an hour to get on the ride.

Operators are fiercely competitive and coy about visitor numbers and profitability for individual parks. Industry estimates, however, put visitor numbers at more than 1 million a year for each of the parks, and observers note that most of the new capital expenditure is coming from free cash flow, not debt.

More than $300 million in development plans are on the drawing board for 1997. This is up to 30 times greater than the $10 million average capital spent each year at Dreamworld.

If approved by the Gold Coast City Council the 1997 plans involve spending an estimated $80 million on developing a 450–room hotel-motel, with 92 treehouses and a themed retail mall, while plans for a $250 million regional shopping centre are expected to be lodged with the council in the first quarter of 1997.

Australian theme parks can achieve a 40 per cent profit before interest and tax, which makes them the most profitable in the world.

Australian Financial Review
31 January 1997

Questions

1. Why is fantasy increasingly regarded as necessary for the new generation of shopping experiences? What sort of fantasy does this mean?

2. What are the implications for the likely development of shopping areas?

3. Why does one market analysis quoted suggest that the retail market will diverge towards the upper and lower quality ranges, leaving mid-range retailers to shrink their store numbers or disappear?

4. What is a 'themed' retail mall, and what do such developments suggest about consumer society?

5. Max Weber was pessimistic about the development of modernity, believing *rationalisation* would lead to *disenchantment* and to a loss of sense of mystery and imagination. Is the blurring of the distinction between theme park and shopping centre something to celebrate, proving Weber wrong, or is it, as Dean McCannell suggests, the end point of consumer capitalism, one which takes away people's imagination and desires, and which then sells them back to them?

OVER TO YOU

Design a participant observation study of a shopping mall, or interview people regarding their experience of theme parks. Decide what themes you want to explore, and how to engage with these through observation and interviews. Write up a report and present it to your tutorial group.

Glossary

Alienation	Experience of being dispossessed of one's creativity by powerful and constraining systems, such as the assembly line.
Androgyny	Blurring of boundaries of masculine and feminine, for example, in popular culture, Michael Jackson.
Anomie	Concept developed by Emile Durkheim to describe the state of individual and social fragmentation and loss of meaning resulting from a society being unable to generate norms.
Biomedical model	Model which conceives of health and illness in terms of functioning of the body, and technological interventions to change this.
Civil society	Field of social and cultural action between the State and the market—made up of associations, social movements, Non-Governmental Organisations etc.
Class consciousness	Awareness of shared experience, culture and interests based on shared class. May overlap with professional identities, local cultures, or shared experience of alienation in work.
Class	Term used to describe social groups defined by a shared relationship to production.
Closure	Ways through which social groups constitute borders to prevent entry and exit.
Commodified	Process of turning dimensions of experience into products which can be bought and sold in a market.
Deinstitutionalisation	The weakening or disappearance of institutions as ways of organising social experience. This implies that society and subjective identity are less and less held together by institutions and their patterns of socialisation.
Deviance	For the functionalist tradition, failure to follow a norm. For the interactionist tradition, the experience of being labelled as different.
Ethnicity	Identity based on identification with a community sharing common culture and history.
Fordism	Concept which emerges out of French regulation school of neo-marxist political economy, but used more broadly to describe the social and cultural patterns of the mass production/mass consumption society.
Functionalism	Sociological tradition associated with Emile Durkheim and Talcott Parsons, premised on idea that we can understand a social experience on the basis of the contribution it makes to social functioning and cohesion. For example, for Durkheim a degree of crime is functional since it allows shared identities to be constructed in opposition to the criminal.

Gender	Socially constructed modes of masculine and feminine experience.
Gentrification	Process of older, often inner-city working class suburbs being repopulated by professionals as older industries are replaced by financial and service industries.
Globalisation	In the context of the weakening of nation states and institutions and of the rise of global flows of information, capital and images, globalisation involves the disconnection of consumer experience, technological and financial flows from any given social organisation—while everywhere, these are not connected to any particular society or culture.
Identity	For sociology, identity is always relational. We construct who we are in relation to other social actors. Actors may have greater or lesser degrees of control over their identity—it may be claimed, or imposed.
Informed consent	Crucial to obtain from people involved in research. For participants in research to give informed consent they must: (1) be aware of the goals of research, (2) be aware that their participation is voluntary and that they may withdraw at any time, (3) they must not be in a relationship of dependence upon the researcher in a way that may prevent their freely choosing to participate or not in the research, (4) they must be aware of any potential risks involved in the research, (5) they must be assured of their anonymity; (6) there must be no adverse consequences to those participating in the research as a result of their participation.
Institution	Form of social organisation constructed in terms of roles, statuses and norms, principal examples being work, family and education. Institutions can be conceived as turning individuals into social beings.
Integration	Refers to the maintenance of social cohesion as opposed to fragmentation. Can be understood in terms of *social* integration, where the emphasis is placed on shared culture and norms (resulting from socialisation) leading social actors to orient their behaviour towards each other. Or can be understood in terms of *system* integration, where society is understood as held together by impersonal mechanisms that work without the awareness of social actors, such as the market, power, or symbolic oppositions to other groups.
Interaction	Approach to social life which sees social life and individual identity as the product of the multitude of exchanges between individuals.
Marginalisation	Experience of being excluded from economic and cultural flows.
Market	System of interaction based on scarcity of resources and competition for those resources.
Medicalisation	Process whereby increasing dimensions of human experience are subject to medical intervention and management.
Moral panic	Construction and mobilisation of shared identity through ritualised opposition to people perceived as in some way violating group norms.

Moralisation	Mode of social regulation where conformity to social norms is understood as a moral imperative.
Normlessness	Social experience where shared definitions of right and wrong break down.
Norms	Social definitions of right and wrong.
Patriarchy	Originally meaning power of the fathers, now used to point to the political, economic and cultural power of men.
Performance	Idea developed by Erving Goffman, that social life consists of drama, and that acting socially involves performance and image management.
Pluralisation	Diversification of lifestyles and values and rise of the culture of tolerance of differences.
Populist	Social and cultural mobilisation of groups defining themselves as 'the people', opposed to elites. Often associated with forms of authoritarianism, or nostalgia for older forms of society.
Postfordism	Concept emerging out of contemporary marxism, based on the idea that decisive technological shifts mean a change in production patterns, such that an older integrated fordist order is giving way to one organised in terms of flexibility, competition and social polarisation between central and periphery workers
Postmodern	A term used in literary and cultural theory. In sociology, it refers to social condition that lacks coherence, and to scepticism towards modern ideologies of progress and linear social development.
Profession	Group whose identity, social status and power are based on the control of knowledge and a claim to self-management and autonomy based on that knowledge.
Rationalisation	For Max Weber, a defining characteristic of modernity. The expansion of a mode of action based on calculations of cost and benefit, and on the search for the most efficient path to achieve goals, leading to a decline in traditional, value-based and emotional dimensions of human experience.
Rite of passage	Ritual marking the transition from one status to another, for example, graduation, marriage.
Ritual	Form of experience which mobilises or expresses shared identity. Examples: Christmas dinner, Anzac Day march.
Role	The action or behaviour associated with status positions.
Role distance	Developed by Erving Goffman, a concept to explain the strategies social actors use in order not to be 'defined' by their role, for example, a waiter serving food in a way that suggests that they know far more about food and drink than their affluent customer.
Sect	Hierarchical group which divides the world into pure and impure.
Secularisation	Decline in religious interpretations of the world and of the place of religion in the organisation of society.
Sick role	A social state, according to Talcott Parsons, which possesses rights and responsibilities and through which society organises the experience of illness.

Social exclusion	Experience of encountering barriers that prevent participating in social, economic and cultural flows, for example, the stigma attached to long-term unemployment.
Social polarisation	Increasing social division and inequality.
Social disorganisation	Breakdown of social structures, such as patterns of authority. Concept first developed by Chicago School of sociologists in 1920s and 1930s to describe dimensions of the immigrant experience.
State	Institutions of government reflecting sovereignty over a territory.
Status	In general use this term denotes degree of prestige—deriving from a conception of social life organised as a hierarchy of honour. For sociologists, however, the term refers to positions that an individual occupies in a social system, for example, lawyer, student, mother. A status is a position that exists in a relationship to other positions, and has roles, or forms of action, attached to it.
Symbolic boundaries	Symbols with which a group defines itself in opposition to others—the symbolic construction of 'them' and 'us'.
Technological determinism	Idea associated with Marxism and spokespersons for globalisation, that technology drives progress, and social life must adapt to the imperatives of technology.
Welfare state	Form of state securing social integration through protection and Keynesian economic management, high or full-employment, and welfare payments, and associated with policies of assimilation of immigrants and indigenous populations.